The Sociable Cook

The Sociable Cook
Katie Stewart

Food photography by Graham Kirk • Wine notes by Stuart Walton

With special thanks to my team at *BBC Homes & Antiques* magazine: Judith Hall, Caroline Wheater and Rebecca Halverson

Published by BBC Worldwide Limited,
Woodlands, 80 Wood Lane,
London, W12 0TT

ISBN 0 563 53772 8

Commissioning Editor: Vivien Bowler
Project Editor: Vicki Vrint
Copy Editor: Christine King
Cover Art Director: Pene Parker
Designer: Janet James
Home economists: Debbie Miller, Julz Berrisford, Kate Jay and Annabel Ford
Stylist: Helen Payne

Set in Bembo and Gill Sans
Printed and bound in Tien Wah Press, Singapore
Colour separations by Kestrel Digital Colour

For information about this and other BBC books, please visit our website on www.bbcshop.com

Contents

The Sociable Cook

Entertaining in your own home is one of life's great pleasures, whether it's an informal lunch or supper, a smart dinner or a buffet to celebrate a special occasion. However, if you've never done it before, or perhaps you're out of practice, it can seem a bit nerve-racking – juggling the food to make sure it's all ready at just the right time while also making your guests feel welcome and relaxed. So the purpose of this book is to give you inspiration and confidence.

The first thing to remember, in this age of microwaved ready meals, is that to entertain your friends with good home cooking is to give them something very special. There is nothing as good as home cooking – it's the best. When the leaves in a salad are fresh and shiny with olive oil, when the juices run pink from your glazed roast duck, when the pastry round a luscious fruit tart crumbles a bit, you have the kind of food to make the mouth water.

The secret of successful entertaining lies in the planning and here my aim has been to do all the hard work for you. The recipes are arranged into menus, each carefully balanced to offer a delicious combination of tastes and texture, and to be easy on the cook. In each case I've included a timeplan so you can see which dishes can be cooked ahead and avoid too much last-minute activity when you want to be greeting your guests. There's no magic art to the cooking itself – it's just a matter of following the recipes, and they are designed to be straightforward. They have all been tested and tasted in my kitchen at home in Sussex – adding a touch more spice here, perhaps another ingredient there; they've been tried out on my friends; and they've been cooked by the readers of *BBC Homes & Antiques* magazine, where these menus first appeared. Among all the letters of appreciation, I've had just one negative comment – that the food was so delicious the portions were too small! (On that particular menu the reader was right and I've adjusted the quantities accordingly.)

I don't believe in unnecessarily complicated recipes, so if a short cut or a ready-made ingredient leads to an end result that tastes just as good, I'll use it. Nor do any of my recipes require ingredients that are difficult to obtain: the spices, herbs and flavourings used are widely available, so please don't think to omit them. They're an essential part of the recipe – as are good ingredients. Be sure to seek out the newest young vegetables for starters or side dishes, the freshest fish, home-produced lamb or local game for a traditional roast or casserole, the choicest fruits for tarts or compotes. Use butter for pastries, good olive oil and wine vinegar, and seasonal produce when it's at its best.

All the recipes have photographs which you can trust as your guide to the finished dishes. Making food look good is part of my job – but I can promise you there's no cheating when mine is photographed! Nor do I like over-decorated food: these days presentation is more to do with the shape, colour and style of the ingredients you choose in the first place than any garnishes added later.

It's all about leaving food looking natural. It's fashionable to serve new young vegetables whole if they are small, and to barely trim them: to leave short green stalks on new carrots and turnips, tails on green beans, skins on new potatoes. On the other hand, cutting vegetables in different ways – on the slant, in slices, grated or diced – can add interest. Leaves can also be used to give a visual lift to food. Herbs are particularly useful: a small sprig of flat-leaf parsley or a few chive stalks on a plate have style; herb leaves look pretty floating in an oil and vinegar dressing; and salad herbs can be left whole among other torn leaves – rocket, baby red chard and mizuna leaves all look good.

There is a vogue for decorating dishes with whole flowers or petals – purple chive flowers, red or yellow nasturtiums and the golden petals of marigolds are pretty. Guests may find whole flowers daunting but petals are always acceptable. Texture is very important and something I look for all the time. Adding a sprinkle of just the right garnish – chopped herbs, coarse pepper from a mill, or a dusting of icing sugar – gives texture to something with a plain surface.

Today's presentation is also about serving food on good-sized platters. Food needs space to look attractive, so think of the plate as its frame. My serving plates are very important to me. I have a much-loved collection of beautiful old large platters and bowls, along with handsome silver serving spoons, that always come out for special occasions. Nothing matches – they're all pieces picked up over the years from antiques and second-hand shops – but that's the way I like it. Overly formal table settings give the wrong atmosphere for really sociable eating.

Like everyone who loves food, I'm always discussing the coming trends and swopping recipe ideas with friends, so I hope the more experienced cooks among you will find a lot of new ideas to try here. And if you're less experienced, it's worth remembering that a recipe is only new the first time that you make it!

Remember too that your friends are coming because they want to see you, to enjoy your and each other's company. The only person who's going to worry about the food is you – and really you needn't. Choose your menu, follow it and relax in the knowledge that the food will taste wonderful. It's your party – enjoy it!

KATIE STEWART

Some practical points

- In the recipes, measurements are given in both metric and imperial. Please use one or the other consistently – mixing the two will fail to give the right result.
- Spoonfuls are level (unless otherwise stated) standard spoon measurements. Cutlery varies so wildly that it's worth buying a set of standard spoon measures (from any cook shop).
- Use large eggs throughout.

Contemporary country cooking

A flavoursome feast

French gourmet dinner

A light classic

A make-ahead spread

Dinner Parties

CONTEMPORARY COUNTRY COOKING

menu for 8

- SPINACH SALAD WITH HOT BACON DRESSING

- BRAISED PHEASANT WITH WILD MUSHROOMS

- AMERICAN WILD RICE AND NUT PILAFF

- HOT BEETROOT WITH BUTTER AND BLACK PEPPER

- WHITE CHOCOLATE RUM BRÛLÉES

A combination of country flavours that complement each other superbly provides the basis for this relaxed dinner menu – perfect for a smart evening with friends who appreciate good food. A salad that mixes crisp, cool spinach leaves and avocado chunks with a hot dressing can be served on individual plates. It must be eaten as soon as it's prepared or the dressing will wilt the delicate salad greens. Gather your leaves, avocado chunks and bacon bits together ahead of time, then prepare this first course with a flourish.

Pheasant is ideal to follow. If you joint the birds, in the same way as you would a chicken, it opens up a whole new range of recipes. Here I've braised the pheasants with seasonal mushrooms. Depending on the time of year you should find wild mushrooms either in

timeplan

The day before

Cook braised pheasant with wild mushrooms – it reheats well. Prepare white chocolate brûlées (except caramel) and refrigerate.

In the morning

Wash salad spinach and refrigerate. Make caramel, break in pieces and tie (airtight) in a polythene bag, so it doesn't go sticky.

1 hour before

Put wild rice and nut pilaff to cook. Decorate white chocolate brûlées. Crisp up bacon bits for salad – remember to reserve bacon drippings.

30–40 minutes before

Put braised pheasant to reheat – low down in oven alongside wild rice pilaff.

Last minute

Heat beetroot with butter and black pepper. Assemble spinach salad.

mixed packs or loose at supermarkets and greengrocers. There are interesting cultivated ones, too; for casseroles or braising, my choice is the dark, flavoursome shiitake mushrooms, which stand up well to slow cooking and have a pretty shape. Leave them whole for effect and, if you like, mix the wild and cultivated sorts. Serve wild rice alongside; it's delicious, goes well with the other flavours and looks good on the table. My pilaff also includes brown basmati rice and toasted flaked almonds for extra crunch. And if you thought beetroot was only good for salads, think again. It makes a stylish and colourful hot accompaniment to pheasant. I buy ready-cooked beetroots in vacuum packs (without vinegar), which saves time and trouble.

Finally, my white chocolate brûlées – a white chocolate mousse with crunchy caramel chips perched on top – are no trouble to make and are always received with rapture.

Spinach salad with hot bacon dressing

You can use a selection of any small salad leaves in this recipe – watercress would be a tasty alternative.

250 g (9 oz) fresh salad
*   spinach*
3 ripe avocados
Juice 1 large lemon
200 g (7 oz) unsmoked back
*   bacon rashers*
4 tablespoons olive oil
1 teaspoon toasted sesame
*   seeds*
Freshly milled pepper

Wash the spinach leaves and dry in a salad spinner or shake in a clean tea cloth. Then enclose the leaves in a roomy polythene bag and refrigerate to keep crisp.

Halve, peel and cut the avocados lengthways and across into chunks and then toss them in the lemon juice.

Trim the rind from the bacon rashers and snip into narrow strips or lardons. Fry the bacon slowly to extract as much fat as possible and allow it to become really crisp. Remove from the pan. Arrange the spinach leaves on the serving plates.

Add the olive oil to the pan drippings, drain the lemon juice from the avocados and add this also. Stir the dressing until hot. Add toasted sesame seeds and season with milled pepper. Scatter the avocado and bacon bits over the spinach leaves. Drizzle over the hot dressing and serve.

Braised pheasant with wild mushrooms

Using pheasant joints overcomes the problem of carving at the table, and braising them means they'll remain tender and not at all dry.

4 pheasants
8–10 shallots
200 g (7 oz) wild mushrooms
   or a mixture with shiitake
   mushrooms
25 g (1 oz) butter
1 tablespoon olive oil
Several sprigs fresh thyme
300 ml (10 fl oz) red wine
400 ml (14 fl oz) vegetable
   stock
1 tablespoon cornflour
3 tablespoons dark soy sauce
2 tablespoons redcurrant jelly
2–3 bay leaves

Cut the legs away from each bird, then slice away the breasts in one piece, from each side of the breastbone, and you will have 8 pheasant breasts and legs. Check them over for any tiny pieces of bone or shot. Peel the shallots, leaving them whole. Pick over the mushrooms, trimming only the ends of the stems to keep the pretty mushroom shapes.

Heat the oven to 180°C/350°F/Gas Mark 4. Melt the butter and oil in a 25 cm (10 in) frying-pan. Add the shallots, and a few pheasant pieces at a time. Turn the pheasant to seal and brown, then transfer to a large 3 litre (5 pint) casserole. As the shallots brown, remove them from the pan and add to the pheasant pieces. Continue until all are in the casserole.

Add the thyme leaves stripped from the stems and all the mushrooms to the hot pan drippings, turn them for a moment or two, then with a slotted spoon transfer to the casserole.

Add the red wine to the hot frying-pan, bring to a simmer, stirring to pick up any flavouring bits, and pour into the casserole. Add the vegetable stock, then the cornflour blended with the soy sauce, the redcurrant jelly and the bay leaves. Cover with the lid. Set in the heated oven and cook for about 1–1½ hours until the pheasant is tender.

Katie's tip

Wild rice is not actually a rice. The slim dark grains are the seeds of an aquatic grass grown in North America. I like to combine wild rice with brown basmati. I buy both separately and mix them to get the proportion of wild to brown rice that I like. You can use packets of ready-mixed wild and brown rice but they are weighted in favour of the less expensive brown rice. Both wild and brown rice need a longer cooking time for the outer bran layer to absorb water and soften – oven cooking is the best way. Choose a casserole with a tight lid to keep in the steam.

American wild rice and nut pilaff

Oven-cooked rice plumps up beautifully and absorbs all the liquid, so there's no need to do any draining; just fork through the nuts and serve.

1 teaspoon salt
250 g (9 oz) wild rice
1 medium onion
50 g (2 oz) butter
250 g (9 oz) brown basmati rice
1.3 litres (2¼ pints) hot vegetable stock
100 g (4 oz) toasted flaked almonds

Heat the oven to 180°C/350°F/Gas Mark 4. Add the salt to 1 litre (1¾ pints) of cold water and bring to the boil. Add the wild rice, stir and simmer for 20 minutes, then drain very thoroughly. Peel and finely chop the onion.

Heat the butter in a 2 litre (3½ pint) flameproof casserole. Add the chopped onion and fry gently to soften. Add the brown rice, stir to coat the grains with the butter and cook for 1 minute. Add the well-drained wild rice and the hot vegetable stock. Bring to a simmer, stirring gently once or twice. Remove from the heat, cover with the casserole lid and transfer to the heated oven. Cook for 45 minutes or until the rice grains are tender and the stock has been absorbed.

Remove the casserole from the oven and let it stand covered for 15 minutes: it will retain its heat. During this time the wild rice grains will pop open. Fork through the almonds and serve.

Hot beetroot with butter and black pepper

This easy recipe gives beetroot a whole new dimension. Plenty of milled black pepper complements its sweet flavour. It is a perfect accompaniment to my braised pheasant, but is delicious served with any game dish.

750 g (1¾ lb) cooked beetroot
50 g (2 oz) butter
Freshly milled black pepper

Cooked whole beetroots will have the skins removed. Simply grate the beetroots on the coarse side of a kitchen grater on to a plate or into a bowl and reserve.

Heat the butter in a medium pan until it has melted and is bubbling. Add the grated beetroot, stirring and tossing it with a fork over a low heat until it is thoroughly heated through – it will take about 5 minutes.

Season well with black pepper – several turns of the pepper mill – and serve.

White chocolate rum brûlées

If you have any small coffee or espresso cups lurking in the china cupboard, get them out for this neat little recipe — the ideal dessert for chocaholics. Keep portions small as this is a rich mixture.

1 x 200 g bar white chocolate, not vanilla-flavoured
1 x 200 ml carton crème fraîche
3 tablespoons dark rum
200 ml (7 fl oz) double cream
50 g (2 oz) granulated sugar

Break the white chocolate into a mixing bowl and set over a pan that is a quarter-filled with hot (not boiling) water until it has melted. Remove the bowl from the heat. Stir in the crème fraîche and then the rum and mix until it is smooth.

In a separate mixing bowl beat the cream to soft peaks. Fold into the chocolate mixture; if the cream doesn't fold in absolutely evenly give a quick stir with a whisk to get a smooth texture. Spoon the mixture into 8 individual ramekin dishes or small coffee cups. Chill in the refrigerator for several hours or overnight and the mixture will set to a delicious mousse texture.

To make the caramel, measure the granulated sugar into a dry pan. Set it over a moderate heat and stir. At first the sugar will form soft clumps, then it will begin to melt and finally turn to a golden caramel.

When it is the right colour, draw the caramel off the heat and pour immediately on to a lightly oiled baking tray — big enough for it to set in a thin layer. As it cools, it will become brittle and a gentle tap will break it in pieces.

Select nicely shaped pieces and perch them on top of the chilled chocolate mixture. Keep chilled until serving time.

Wine recommendations

The salad may seem a light enough starter, but remember that avocado has a fatty texture and will need a wine with a cutting-edge of fresh, youthful acidity to throw it into relief. A well-made, crisp Italian white of the most recent vintage, such as Frascati or the less well-known Arneis from Piedmont, would do the trick, or you might opt for something like a dry Vouvray from the Loire. The traditional vinous partner for a game bird is burgundy, and if the budget permits, a raspberry-scented Beaune or Pommard would be impeccable. Otherwise, try one of the New Zealand or Chilean Pinot Noirs for the same weight and range of flavours. The dessert needs a rich, botrytized sweet wine (i.e. one that has had its sugars concentrated by allowing the grapes to rot on the vine), ideally from the Sémillon grape, from Australia or California.

A FLAVOURSOME FEAST

menu for 8

- WARM SCALLOP SALAD
- PEPPERED BEEF FILLET
- MUSTARD-GLAZED ONIONS
- BOULANGÈRE POTATOES
- SAFFRON PEARS WITH ORANGE AND RUM SAUCE

This is a dinner party menu of delicious food, simply cooked and with wonderful flavours. It does involve a bit of last-minute activity, but it's worth it. Have everything measured and set out ready, and last-minute preparation is a straightforward assembly job. For the starter I have chosen a warm salad of stir-fried scallops with a sweet chilli dressing. Arrange the leaves attractively on serving plates, then add the scallops. The visual effect is all-important, so make sure the scallops glisten with the chilli dressing.

Peppered beef fillet is reliably tender to serve for the main dish and there's nothing to the recipe. What's important here is the quality of your beef; it must have the flavour that comes with a piece of meat that is well bred (preferably Scottish) and well hung. I'd be fussy on

this occasion and ask the butcher to cut the piece from a whole fillet. I have worked out a gravy mix that can sit in a bowl and only needs adding to the roasting tin for a swift simmer before serving. Mustard-glazed onions will be perfect with the beef. The best partner for these robust flavours would be sliced potatoes cooked in stock; tender and mild tasting, they have an extra advantage in that you can get them cooked and ready beforehand – then they only need a crisp-up so that the top layer browns attractively.

I can't resist choosing pears for dessert; they are so elegant and stylish. Simmered in a saffron syrup and served with orange and rum sauce, these pears have the most extraordinary colour – they come up bright yellow, to look every bit as good as they taste.

The day before

Prepare salad greens for warm scallop salad, then tie in a polythene bag and refrigerate; make chilli dressing. Poach pears in saffron syrup and make orange and rum sauce; let both cool and refrigerate.

Early on the day

Prepare and bake sliced potatoes to the first stage, cool but do not refrigerate. Peel small onions. Assemble saffron pears with orange rum sauce and chill. Prepare beef fillet and leave to marinate at room temperature.

30 minutes before

Put beef fillet to cook. Prepare mustard-glazed onions. Put sliced potatoes in to brown.

Last minute

Prepare warm scallop salad and serve.

Warm scallop salad

Fresh scallops stir-fried and served warm, with a sweet chilli-flavoured
dressing and a few green leaves, make a delicious starter.

150 g (5 oz) salad herb
* leaves*
½ cucumber
1 bunch spring onions
2 tablespoons grapeseed oil
16 fresh scallops (roe
* attached)*

For the sweet chilli dressing

3 tablespoons lemon juice
1 tablespoon Thai fish sauce
2 tablespoons sweet (not hot)
* chilli sauce*
1 tablespoon soft brown sugar
Salt and freshly milled pepper
150 ml (5 fl oz) grapeseed oil
1 teaspoon dried chilli flakes

Rinse the salad herb leaves and shake dry. Peel and thinly slice the
cucumber. Trim the spring onions and slice lengthways. Combine
the salad ingredients and refrigerate until serving time, then
distribute salad leaves and cucumber between each serving plate –
reserve the spring onions for a garnish. For the sweet chilli
dressing, combine the lemon (or lime) juice, Thai fish sauce, sweet
chilli sauce, brown sugar and a seasoning of salt and milled pepper.
Add the oil and chilli flakes and stir to mix.

Heat 2 tablespoons of grapeseed oil in a 25 cm (10 in) frying-
pan. Add the scallops and stir-fry for 1–2 minutes – scallops
tenderize quickly and will turn opaque; they will also brown a
little. Take the pan off the heat and, with a slotted spoon, transfer
the scallops to the salad plates, allowing two per serving. Add sweet
chilli dressing to the hot pan, and stir. Spoon the warm dressing
over the salad, add a spring onion garnish and serve.

Peppered beef fillet

This recipe couldn't be easier – a piece of beef fillet, flash roasted and served medium rare, in thick slices.

1 kg (2¼ lb) piece beef fillet
2 tablespoons olive oil
2 tablespoons cracked pepper

For the pepper gravy
250 ml (8 fl oz) red wine
200 ml (7 fl oz) vegetable stock
1 tablespoon redcurrant jelly
1 teaspoon cracked pepper

Rub the meat with the olive oil, then rub cracked pepper over the surface. Leave to marinate for 3 hours at room temperature – if chilled, it alters the cooking time.

Measure the red wine for the gravy into a pan, bring it to the boil then simmer for 10 minutes to reduce and concentrate the wine flavour; check the quantity – there should be 100 ml (3½ fl oz) of wine remaining. Combine with the vegetable stock, redcurrant jelly and the cracked pepper in a bowl and refrigerate.

Heat the oven to 230°C/450°F/Gas Mark 8. Calculate the cooking time, allowing 15 minutes per 500 g (1 lb 2 oz). Put the beef fillet in a roasting tin, set in the heated oven and roast for 30 minutes, until the fillet has a nice brown crust and is medium rare inside. Transfer meat to a carving board and leave for 10–15 minutes. Set the roasting tin over a direct heat, add the contents of the gravy bowl, stir and bring to a simmer.

Cut the beef fillet in thick slices, allowing two per person, and arrange on a heated platter. Add any juices from the carving board to the gravy, then drizzle over meat slices and serve.

Katie's tip
Cracked pepper comprises coarsely broken black peppercorns that provide a delicious hot flavour. It is often used as an extra flavour pressed over the surface of meat. You could crush whole peppercorns in a pestle and mortar but I think it's better to buy it: you might find it labelled 'steak pepper' on the supermarket spice shelf.

Mustard-glazed onions

Baby onions are the ones to choose when serving onions as a vegetable side dish. A mustard flavour works well in this recipe, and these onions are excellent with steak and roast beef.

1 kg (2¼ lb) baby onions
75 g (3 oz) butter
3 tablespoons prepared
  English mustard
Salt and freshly milled pepper
2 tablespoons chopped parsley

Peel the onions, leaving them whole. The best way to deal with small onions is to take a thin slice off the top and bottom of each, put them together in a bowl and cover with boiling water from the kettle, then leave them for 5 minutes before draining. Now you will find that the outer skins slip off quite easily.

Place the onions in a pan and cover with cold, salted water. Bring to the boil and simmer for 20–30 minutes or until tender – test with a knife tip – then drain.

Add the butter to the hot pan and allow it to melt. Stir in the mustard, then add the onions. Toss to coat the onions in the butter and mustard glaze. Season with salt and freshly milled pepper and stir in the chopped parsley.

Boulangère potatoes

Here's a simple but delicious way to cook potatoes; the unobtrusive flavour makes an excellent contrast to the peppery heat of the beef fillet.

1.5 kg (3 lb) maincrop
  potatoes
75 g (3 oz) butter
Salt and freshly milled pepper
300 ml (10 fl oz) hot
  vegetable stock

Heat the oven to 190°C/375°F/Gas Mark 5. Peel the potatoes and cut into even slices a little under 5 mm (¼ in) thick – a mandolin slicer is useful here. Using about 25 g (1 oz) of the butter, generously grease the inside of a 1.5 litre (2½ pint) baking dish – choose one that is shallow rather than deep for lots of crispy top.

Arrange layers of sliced potato in the buttered dish, sprinkling them with salt and milled pepper and flakes of a further 25 g (1 oz) of the butter. Finish with a layer of potatoes neatly arranged. Pour in the vegetable stock until it barely reaches the top layer of potato slices – do not cover the potatoes with stock. Cover the dish with buttered greaseproof paper. Set in the heated oven and bake until the potatoes are tender and the stock has almost

evaporated – about 45 minutes – and test with the tip of a knife.
Up to this stage you can prepare these potatoes beforehand.

Remove the protective paper covering and brush the top layer
of potato slices with the remaining butter, melted. Return the
potatoes to the oven and cook for 15–20 minutes until hot and
the top layer is crisp and golden brown. Rather than serve these
potatoes in the baking dish, I prefer to spoon them into a heated
serving dish.

Saffron pears with orange and rum sauce

Choose plump pears that will stand upright easily for this recipe –
Comice or Rocha would be good choices.

*175 g (6 oz) granulated
    sugar
Generous pinch saffron
    strands
2–3 pieces pared lemon rind
8 firm dessert pears*

For the orange sauce

*50 g (2 oz) granulated sugar
1 tablespoon cornflour
350 ml (12 fl oz) fresh
    orange juice
2 tablespoons dark rum*

For the candied peel

*2 oranges
2 tablespoons caster sugar*

Choose a pan large enough for these pears to lie snugly and in a single layer – they must be under the syrup to take the colour. Put the sugar and saffron strands in the pan and, using the back of a wooden spoon, crush the saffron strands with the sugar to break them up. Add 600 ml (1 pint) cold water and the pared lemon rind and bring to a simmer, stirring to dissolve the sugar. Peel the pears, leaving them whole; drop them into the pan of syrup. Bring to a simmer and poach for 30–40 minutes or until tender. Leave the pears to cool in the syrup overnight.

For the orange sauce, combine the sugar and cornflour in a saucepan and stir in the measured orange juice. Bring to the boil, and stir until thickened. Draw off the heat and add dark rum. Let the sauce cool, stirring occasionally to prevent a skin forming.

For the candied orange peel garnish, start by paring the rind from the oranges using a vegetable peeler. Shred the rind into thin strips and blanch in boiling water to cover for 5 minutes to tenderize, then drain. Put the caster sugar and 150 ml (5 fl oz) cold water into another pan and heat, stirring, to make a syrup. Add the blanched orange rind and simmer for 4–5 minutes until candied. Lift the peel from the syrup and allow to cool.

Lift the pears from the syrup and place in a serving bowl. Discard the cooking syrup. Spoon over the orange rum sauce and add a garnish of candied peel.

Wine recommendations

The natural sweetness of scallops suggests a first-course wine with a corresponding hint of residual sugar in it. German Riesling of Kabinett or Spätlese level would be superb, or you could try one of the weightier examples from Australia. Clare Valley is among the best regions for Riesling down under. A burly red with good spicy edge and a moderate amount of tannin is what peppered beef needs. Look to the Rhône Valley, perhaps Crozes-Hermitage or Gigondas, for wines in this style, or try a muscularly built Australian Grenache. An equally sturdy sweet wine is required to cope with the sauce on those pears. Orange Muscat and Flora from Australia has the right amount of oomph, and will match the orange used in the dish.

FRENCH GOURMET DINNER

menu for 6

- TOMATO TARTS WITH BASIL
- PROVENÇAL ROAST MONKFISH
- WHITE BEANS WITH BUTTER AND CREAM
- SPINACH MOULDS
- CHOCOLATE MARQUISE WITH CHOCOLATE SAUCE AND APRICOTS

For the smart occasion, a formal dinner menu with a French theme. The emphasis here is on interesting combinations of flavour and elegant presentation. Delicious, hot puff-pastry tomato tarts with basil start the meal. Made as individual servings, they can be prepared ahead and baked to serve.

Monkfish, although expensive, is delicious and meaty. The idea of roasting a large piece of fish is typically simple and unpretentious – something I like about French cooking. Ask your fishmonger for advice; the very thick fillets that come from the head end of the fish can often be roasted as they are, while the thinner tail-end fillets tied together make a better-looking joint. I think monkfish really does need a garlic flavour but, rather than stud the flesh with garlic slivers, which is the

usual way, I've roasted heads of garlic separately so guests can make their own choice. Serve the fish, roasted garlic heads and the pretty spinach moulds on a handsome serving platter and pass around the floury, cooked haricot beans to soak up the roasted fish juices.

I am very much in favour of the French style of serving a light salad after the main dish – just mixed leaves turned in good olive oil with milled sea salt and coarse black pepper, nothing more – then a sliver of soft cheese before dessert. This allows guests to finish off the wine and clears the palate for a stunning dessert. My recipe for a chocolate marquise should prove irresistible; the rich chocolate loaf has a smooth dense texture, somewhere between a light silky mousse and chocolate fudge. The perfect note on which to end.

timeplan

The day before
Soak and cook haricot beans. Make chocolate marquise and refrigerate. Prepare chocolate sauce and glazed apricots.

In the morning
Prepare tomato tarts and chill. Prepare spinach moulds and refrigerate. Marinate monkfish.

1 hour before
Turn out and finish chocolate marquise.

30–40 minutes before
Finish recipe for white beans. Put garlic heads on to roast for monkfish. Bake and serve tarts.

15–25 minutes before serving main course
Put monkfish on to roast. Set spinach moulds to cook.

Tomato tarts with basil

Use ready-rolled puff pastry – it's easy and looks so professional.

*375 g pack ready-rolled puff
  pastry*
*500 g (1 lb 2 oz) medium-
  sized ripe tomatoes*
Beaten egg to glaze
Salt and freshly milled pepper
2 tablespoons pesto sauce
1–2 tablespoons olive oil
Fresh basil for garnish

Cut out six 7.5 cm (3 in) circles of pastry with a floured cutter.
Chill the circles between sheets of greaseproof paper. Cut away the
core from each tomato and score the skins. Scald in boiling water
for 1 minute, then plunge into cold water and peel off the skins.
Cut each tomato in half vertically and scoop out seeds and juice.
Then cut the halves in half again to make four 'petals' from each.

Arrange the pastry circles on an ungreased baking tray. Prick
all over with a fork, then brush with the egg. Then, on each base,
arrange a circle of overlapping tomato petals – you will need 6 for
each tart. Chill until needed.

Heat the oven to 200°C/400°F/Gas Mark 6. Place the tarts on
a baking tray, season with salt and pepper and bake for 15–20
minutes. Thin the pesto sauce with a little olive oil, then drizzle
over the hot tarts. Add fresh basil leaves and serve.

Provençal roast monkfish

Each monkfish tail should serve three people. Ask your fishmonger to keep the fillets from the tails in pairs so that you can tie them together easily for a better-looking joint.

*2 monkfish tails about
   700–900 g (1½–2 lb)
   each, skinned and with the
   fillets taken off the bone*
5 tablespoons olive oil
1 teaspoon cracked pepper
3–4 heads garlic
50 g (2 oz) butter
Salt and freshly milled pepper
Rind and juice 1 lemon
*3 tablespoons chopped flatleaf
   parsley*
*100 ml (3½ fl oz) dry white
   wine*
12 black olives

Tie each pair of monkfish tails with fine string to reshape. Rub the prepared joints of fish with 3 tablespoons of olive oil and the cracked pepper and marinate in the refrigerator for 2–4 hours.

Heat the oven to 200°C/400°F/Gas Mark 6. Place the garlic heads on an oven shelf and roast for 30–40 minutes. Melt the butter and remaining olive oil in a 25 cm (10 in) frying-pan. Add the monkfish tails (best side down) and let them brown. Transfer the monkfish (right side up) to a hot roasting tin and season. Drizzle over the juices from the pan and transfer to the oven. Roast the monkfish for 20 minutes, basting it occasionally.

Transfer the fish to a serving platter and scatter with lemon zest and parsley. To the pan juices, add the lemon juice and wine. Bring to a simmer, stirring well. Season, then spoon the juices over the fish. Add the olives and garlic to the platter.

To serve, snip the string and remove, then separate the fish fillets and break each into 3 portions. Tear the garlic heads open.

Katie's tip

Garlic takes on a more gentle flavour and doesn't linger on the breath when roasted – the flesh inside the papery skins softens to a purée. To roast, put the garlic heads directly on to the oven rack – they can go alongside other items – and test by pressing gently. They feel soft when ready and should be served hot. To eat, simply press each clove with a fork to squeeze out the soft flesh.

White beans with butter and cream

Floury haricot beans are in keeping with the French theme here, but a creamed potato purée would do well too.

350 g (12 oz) haricot beans
2 medium onions, cut into
*   thin rings*
50 g (2 oz) butter
1 tablespoon olive oil
2 bay leaves
1 teaspoon caster sugar
Salt and freshly milled pepper
2 teaspoons white wine
*   vinegar*
150 ml (5 fl oz) double
*   cream*

Cover the unsoaked beans with cold water, bring them slowly to the boil and simmer for 5 minutes only. Cover with the pan lid and leave them to soak for 1 hour, then drain. Re-cover with cold water, bring to the boil again, then lower the heat and simmer for 30–40 minutes or until the beans are tender, then drain and put in the refrigerator until needed.

Prepare the onions. Heat the butter and oil in a large pan. Add the onion rings and bay leaves and sprinkle with the sugar. Cook gently for 8–10 minutes or until the onions are soft. Add the beans to the pan and stir to coat them with the buttery onion juices. Season well and add the wine vinegar. Stir in the double cream and check the seasoning. Bring to a simmer just before serving.

Spinach moulds

Large leaves of spinach are wrapped around a creamy spinach mixture and baked in small dariole moulds. They are well protected in the covered moulds, so you can put them under the monkfish.

500 g (1 lb 2 oz) fresh
*   spinach (buy large spinach*
*   leaves – not salad spinach)*
25 g (1 oz) butter
25 g (1 oz) plain flour
300 ml (10 fl oz) milk
Salt and freshly milled pepper
3 eggs
2 tablespoons double cream
Grated nutmeg

Tear away the coarse stems of the spinach and wash the leaves in cold water. Reserve about 8–10 of the best large leaves. Lift the rest from the water and pack them into a pan. Cover and cook over a moderate heat until soft – the leaves provide sufficient liquid, so don't add water. Drain well, pressing out excess water, and purée in a food processor.

Melt the butter over a low heat, stir in the flour and cook for a moment. Gradually beat in the milk, stirring well. Bring to the boil, season and cook for 2–3 minutes. Draw off the heat and cool for a moment. Add the white sauce, eggs, cream and nutmeg to the spinach purée and mix in the food processor again to make

creamed spinach. Scald the remaining spinach leaves in a colander with boiling water from the kettle and press flat on kitchen paper. Line 6 buttered moulds with the leaves, pour in the creamed spinach to fill, and turn in the overlapping leaves over the filling. Chill until time to cook.

Heat the oven to 190°C/375°F/Gas Mark 5. Set the spinach moulds in a large tin and add boiling water to a depth of 2.5 cm (1 in). Cover with foil. Set in the heated oven and bake for 15–20 minutes. Lift the moulds from the pan, cool for 5 minutes, then turn out and serve.

Chocolate marquise with chocolate sauce and apricots

Anything chocolatey tastes good and looks pretty served with fruit –
whether it's sliced strawberries or my choice of glazed apricots.

*250 g (9 oz) Continental
plain chocolate (e.g. a good
quality bittersweet variety)*
100 g (4 oz) unsalted butter
*175 g (6 oz) icing sugar,
sifted*
3 eggs
*1 teaspoon instant coffee
granules, dissolved in
1 teaspoon boiling water*

For the chocolate sauce
100 g (4 oz) caster sugar
50 g (2 oz) cocoa

For the glazed apricots
*175 g (6 oz) 'ready-to-eat'
dried apricots*
*150 g (5 oz) granulated
sugar*
3 tablespoons rum

For the decoration
Chocolate shavings and cocoa

Line a small 20 x 10 x 5 cm (8 x 4 x 2 in) oblong loaf pan with clear film, allowing it to overlap the edges. Break the chocolate into a bowl and set over a pan of hot (not boiling) water until melted. Stir until smooth and remove from the heat.

In a bowl, cream the butter and icing sugar until smooth. Separate the eggs, beating the yolks into the creamed butter one at a time. Beat in the coffee mixture, add the melted chocolate and mix well. Whisk the egg whites until stiff and fold into the chocolate mixture. Spoon into the loaf pan and spread evenly. Turn in the clear film edges to cover, and chill until firm for at least 4 hours or overnight.

For the chocolate sauce, measure 150 ml (5 fl oz) cold water and the sugar into a pan. Stir over a low heat until the sugar is dissolved and bring to the boil. Add the cocoa all at once and whisk until smooth. Bring back to a simmer and draw off the heat. Cool, then chill until serving time.

To make the glazed apricots, measure 200 ml (7 fl oz) cold water into a pan, add the apricots and bring to a simmer, cover and cook gently for 10 minutes. Add the sugar, stir until it has dissolved, then bring to a simmer and draw off the heat before adding the rum. Cover and leave at room temperature overnight. Use a little of the syrup to serve with the apricots.

Before serving, invert the marquise on to a plate, discard the wrappings and let it stand for 1 hour at room temperature. Add the chocolate shavings and dust with cocoa. Cut into slices and spoon on the chocolate sauce, apricots and syrup.

 Wine recommendations

With the tomato tarts, you will need a crisp, dry white with sufficient acidity to stand up to what can otherwise be a tricky flavour for wine. Sauvignon Blanc wines are especially well equipped to deal with tomato. Good ones come from the Loire (the best are Pouilly-Fumé or Sancerre), the Marlborough area of New Zealand's South Island, or from Stellenbosch or Paarl in South Africa. Proceed then to a richer, fatter white with the monkfish, one that has a modicum of oak-ageing on it. White Rioja Crianza or one of the oakier Chardonnay wines from the Languedoc would make appropriate matches. Choose an Australian botrytized (see page 18) dessert wine for the chocolate marquise, either a Riesling or a Sémillon. They're widely available in half-bottles, and are exceptionally good value.

A LIGHT CLASSIC

This simple menu is light and tasty – and ideal for any gathering of family and friends. Almost everyone likes fresh salmon and it's such a straightforward fish to cook. For this occasion, I have prepared it with a deliciously crisp puff pastry crust.

For the recipe you will need a tail piece separated into two fillets. My advice is to buy your fish from the fishmonger and let him do all the preparation for you. Wrapping a salmon in pastry is well worth doing when there's a crowd. It must be puff pastry because it's so flaky and crisp – a lovely contrast to the delicate texture of the salmon. Slotting tarragon butter (especially tasty with salmon) between the fish fillets keeps the flesh moist. Serve thick slices with my hot watercress sauce, attractively flecked with green.

Get out a decorative platter for the vegetables – it's such a pretty way to serve them. Mini-vegetables such as cauliflowers are charming; add small new potatoes and asparagus spears or green beans but don't crowd the platter with too much choice. A mustard vinaigrette to spoon over the hot vegetables makes a great flavour combination, or you could go for melted lemon butter – the choice is yours.

For dessert I've chosen a colourful salad of exotic fruits in a spiced syrup with almond cakes. Remember that the syrup will appear quite sweet until the fruits are added so it is important let the mixture marinate for several hours. Come serving time, the sweet syrup will have drawn out the natural fruit juices and achieved a perfect balance of flavours.

timeplan

The day before

Bake almond cakes and store in airtight container when cool. Make syrup for exotic fruits.

In the morning

Prepare salmon, wrap in pastry, cover with cling film and refrigerate. Cut up fruits and marinate in syrup. Prepare vegetables. Mix dressing or measure butter into pan for lemon butter. Make watercress sauce; leave to cool, stir to prevent skin forming, cover with cling film and refrigerate.

I hour before

Bake the salmon.

Last minute

Steam and simmer vegetables and arrange on platter. Melt butter for vegetables, if using. Reheat watercress sauce.

Salmon in puff pastry

Not for me the usual pastry 'fish' with pastry scales! Instructions here are for a more interesting and unusual way to wrap a piece of salmon – and it's easier to slice and serve too.

1 tail piece of salmon, about 1.5 kg (3 lb), separated into 2 fillets, with skin removed
Salt and freshly milled pepper
6–8 sprigs fresh tarragon
75 g (3 oz) butter, at room temperature
1 x 375 g pack ready-rolled fresh puff pastry
Beaten egg to seal and glaze
Coarse sea-salt flakes to decorate the pastry

Lay the salmon fillets flesh side up on a chopping board. Run your fingers along the flesh from head to tail to check for any small stray fish bones and tweeze them out. Season with salt and pepper.

Strip the tarragon leaves from the stems and chop the leaves finely. Mash the butter and tarragon together until well mixed. Dot the tarragon butter in flakes along the flesh side of one fillet. Place the second fillet on top, flesh side down, matching head ends with tail ends so that the fish piece is squared off.

Unroll the pastry and place it on a lightly floured surface. Roll the pastry to extend it to a shape that will enclose the fish – mine required a piece 35 cm (14 in) square. Trim the edges of the pastry straight with a kitchen knife, then cut the pastry into two lengths – one slightly narrower to go under the fish and the second wider to go over the top. My lengths were 16 cm (6½ in) and 19 cm (7½ in) wide. Transfer the narrower length on to an ungreased baking tray sprinkled with a few drops of cold water. Place the prepared fish on top and dampen the pastry border all round with a little beaten egg.

Prepare the second pastry piece as follows. Fold the pastry in half lengthways. Using a kitchen knife (dipped in flour before each cut), cut a series of narrow strips from the folded side of the pastry, leaving a 2.5 cm (1 in) uncut border on the opposite side and at each end. Open the piece of pastry out over the fish and press around the uncut border to seal it against the pastry underneath the fish. Cover the fish with cling film and refrigerate – you can prepare it 4–6 hours in advance.

Heat the oven to 190°C/375°F/Gas Mark 5. Brush the pastry lattice and border with beaten egg, then scatter with a little sea salt to decorate and add texture. Bake for 45 minutes or until the pastry is golden and the salmon cooked. Push a knife tip through one of the lattice slits to test – the salmon flesh should flake. Transfer the salmon to a heated platter and let it settle for 10 minutes. Slice thickly in portions and serve with the hot watercress sauce.

Watercress sauce

A creamy white sauce with lots of green flecks, this is delicious with hot poached or baked salmon or trout.

1 x 85 g pack fresh watercress
300 ml (10 fl oz) vegetable
*   stock*
40 g (1½ oz) butter
2 level tablespoons flour
Salt and freshly milled pepper
Grated nutmeg
150 ml (5 fl oz) single cream

Pinch the tops and leaves from the watercress and chop them finely. Lightly crush a small bunch of the watercress stalks. Place the vegetable stock in a pan, add the stalks, heat to simmering, then remove from the heat. Infuse for 10–15 minutes, then strain and discard the stalks.

Melt the butter over a low heat, stir in the flour and cook gently for 1 minute. Gradually pour in the warm stock, stirring well to get a smooth sauce, and bring to a simmer. Season with salt, pepper and nutmeg. Simmer gently for 2–3 minutes. Add cream and watercress leaves and warm through.

Hot vegetable platter

I like to steam vegetables but, for speed, it's best to simmer some and steam others. Serve hot with mustard vinaigrette or melted lemon butter.

250 g (9 oz) fine green beans
450 g (1 lb) thin asparagus
4 mini cauliflowers or
*   1 medium cauliflower*
500 g (1 lb 2 oz) new
*   potatoes*

For the dressing either:
200 ml (7 fl oz) prepared oil
*   and vinegar dressing*
2 tablespoons grainy mustard

Or:
100 g (4 oz) unsalted butter
Small piece pared lemon rind
Freshly milled pepper

Your combination of vegetables can be whatever suits you, and you can include just a few or as many as you can reasonably cook. Trim the stalk ends from the beans but leave on the tails – they look good. Cut about 2.5 cm (1 in) from long asparagus stalks. Trim the mini cauliflowers but leave the pretty inner green leaves; if using a medium cauliflower, cut the head into quarters. Scrub the potatoes, leaving on the skins.

In a roomy frying-pan of simmering salted water first cook the green beans (for 6–8 minutes), lift from the pan with a slotted spoon, then add the asparagus (for 8 minutes). At the same time, steam the potatoes (for 10 minutes), then the cauliflower (for 8–10 minutes). When all the vegetables are cooked, transfer them to a colander and cover to keep warm. Meanwhile stir up the oil and

vinegar dressing with the mustard and taste. Or melt the butter
and add the lemon rind and freshly milled pepper; when hot, pour
into a warm serving bowl, leaving the white sediment behind.
Arrange the vegetables in groups on a hot platter and serve with
vinaigrette or butter.

Exotic fruits in spiced syrup

Stand the bowl of fruit at room temperature for a couple of hours for added flavour to develop before serving.

900 g (2 lb) prepared exotic fruits: 1 x 340 g tub fresh pineapple chunks, 1 ripe mango, 1 papaya, 250 g (9 oz) red seedless grapes, 3 kiwi fruit and 1 star fruit

For the syrup
175 g (6 oz) golden granulated sugar
1 cinnamon stick, broken in half
6 slices fresh ginger
6–8 whole green cardamom pods
Pared rind and juice 1 lime
2 tablespoons dark rum

To make the syrup, measure the sugar into a pan with 200 ml (7 fl oz) water. Add the cinnamon and ginger – slice across a piece of fresh ginger; there's no need to peel it. Remove the seeds from the cardamom pods, crush them lightly and add to the pan along with the lime rind. Stir over a low heat to dissolve the sugar, bring to a simmer for 5 minutes, then remove from the heat and leave to infuse until cold. If you can, let the syrup stand for a further 3–4 hours, or even overnight, and it will take more flavour from the spices and become quite gingery. Add the lime juice and rum.

Prepare the fruits and place in a serving bowl. Peel, remove seeds or stones and cut into large chunks. Strain the spiced syrup over the fruit and return the cinnamon to the bowl for decorative effect. Allow the fruits to marinate for 3–4 hours before serving.

Katie's tip

To cut a mango into neat chunks, first you need to locate the large flat stone running lengthways along the centre. To do this, roll your mango on a table and it will settle with the stone sitting horizontally. With a sharp knife, cut two slices either side of the stone, against the flat edges. Now criss-cross the flesh of the mango on both halves and push up from underneath so that the flesh pops up concave. Then you can cut away the chunks of fruit.

Almond cakes

Little dessert cakes that are just two-bite-sized are perfect for serving with marinated fruits – encourage your guests to dip them in the spicy syrup.

Makes 24

75 g (3 oz) self-raising flour
50 g (2 oz) ground almonds
100 g (4 oz) butter
100 g (4 oz) caster sugar
Grated rind 1 lemon
2 eggs
2–3 drops almond essence
50–75 g (2–3 oz) flaked
  almonds
Icing sugar, to serve

Heat the oven to 180°C/350°F/Gas Mark 4. Brush two 12-cup tartlet trays with melted butter.

Sift the flour on to a square of greaseproof paper and add the ground almonds. In a mixing bowl, cream the butter, sugar and lemon rind. In another bowl, lightly mix the eggs and almond essence with a fork. Gradually beat the egg into the creamed mixture, then fold in the flour.

Drop a heaped teaspoon of the cake mixture into each cup in the prepared tins. Top generously with flaked almonds and bake for 15 minutes. Remove the trays from the oven and place on a damp teacloth to loosen the undersides of the cakes. Leave for 2–3 minutes, then loosen the sides and turn out. Cool and dust with icing sugar.

Wine recommendations

Salmon is remarkably versatile when it comes to choosing wine, and is surprisingly good with a light, mildly chilled red such as Pinot Noir or one of the lighter wines from the Beaujolais region – perhaps Brouilly. Equally, a well-made, fruit-scented rosé from somewhere like southern France, Australia or Chile can be excellent, and would make a good lunchtime choice. However, the watercress sauce would incline me towards a white here and one with a certain amount of citric tang. Think Sémillon or Riesling from Australia, or New Zealand Sauvignon. Only the most delicate wine will suit the fruit dessert. German Riesling Auslese would work, but you might be better off with a slightly sweet sparkler such as demi-sec champagne.

A MAKE-AHEAD SPREAD

menu for 10

- TWICE-BAKED SPINACH SOUFFLÉS
- HONEY-GLAZED DUCK IN GRAPEFRUIT AND GINGER SAUCE
- POT-ROASTED NEW POTATOES P.48
- FRENCH-STYLE PEAS
- CHOCOLATE RUM CAKE WITH RED FRUIT SAUCE

A family celebration is the perfect excuse for a spot of entertaining. Whether it's a birthday or perhaps a wedding anniversary that you're honouring, there's nothing nicer than having guests around your own dinner table. Lavish party menus can be daunting but take heart – the recipes I've chosen can be mostly prepared the day before.

Right now, it's fashionable to start a dinner party by serving single hot canapés with pre-dinner drinks; nothing too substantial – there's no need for more than two bites per person. Buy in something that you can warm through moments before – a choice of mini quiches or a selection of cocktail crostini – to get everyone in the party mood.

Twice-baked soufflé is a classic dish that can easily be prepared ahead ready for a final bake and serve. Light and elegant, these mini soufflés are spinach-flavoured

timeplan

The day before

Bake chocolate cake layer
and soak in rum syrup.
Make basic red fruit sauce
and chill. Bake spinach
soufflés, arrange in gratin
dish and chill.

In the morning

Make grapefruit and
ginger sauce for duck. Rub
duck breasts with honey
glaze and chill. Top cake
layer with cream and chill.

I–2 hours before

Take soufflés from
refrigerator. Rinse new
potatoes and assemble
in casserole. Dust cake
with cocoa powder –
keep chilled. Add
strawberries to red
fruit sauce and leave at
room temperature.

40 minutes before

Put duck to roast and
add grapefruit to sauce and
warm. Bake new potatoes
on shelf below duck.
Assemble peas and cook.

Last minute

Reheat soufflés for serving.

and sprinkled with Parmesan. The availability of good
plump duck breasts makes roast duck an excellent main
dish choice. I like the Gressingham duck breasts for their
superb flavour and good size. Roast duck goes well with
anything tangy; my choice is grapefruit, with fruit
segments served in a sauce made with fresh ginger. Peas
and new potatoes are the traditional accompaniments
for roast duck and I see nothing wrong with that. Here,
though, both are cooked in intriguing ways. The peas
are sweet and pretty with the added texture of spring
onions and Cos lettuce. New potatoes are particularly
delicious pot-roasted in a casserole and then tossed with
sea salt and coarsely milled pepper,

   A melt-in-the-mouth dessert cake is the perfect
gourmet finale for a celebration party. This one
combines chocolate, rum and red fruits – the flavours
marry beautifully and the texture is soft and moist.

Twice-baked spinach soufflés

The obvious advantage of twice-baked soufflés is that they can be made the day before. These spinach soufflés reheat perfectly, with a light texture and excellent flavour.

For the soufflés

*500 g (1 lb 2 oz) fresh
    spinach*
50 g (2 oz) butter
40 g (1½ oz) plain flour
300 ml (10 fl oz) milk
*Salt and freshly milled black
    pepper*
Grated nutmeg
6 eggs
*300 ml (10 fl oz) double
    cream*
50 g (2 oz) grated Parmesan

You will need an extra
25 g (I oz) melted butter
and 2–3 tablespoons of
grated Parmesan to prepare
the ramekins.

Detach the spinach leaves, rinse in cold water and lift straight into a large pan. Set over a moderate heat, cover – don't add extra water – and cook for 2–3 minutes until the spinach wilts. Drain in a colander, pressing well. When spinach has cooled, squeeze firmly to extract excess water and chop finely.

Heat the oven to 180°C/350°F/Gas Mark 4. Brush 10 small ramekin dishes with melted butter and sprinkle with Parmesan. Melt the butter for the soufflés in a medium pan, stir in the flour and cook over a moderate heat for a few minutes. Slowly add the milk, beating to make a smooth sauce. Bring to a simmer and cook for 2–3 minutes. Add seasoning and a good grating of nutmeg, then remove the sauce from the heat and let it cool slightly. Separate the eggs, reserving the whites and beating the yolks into the sauce. Stir in the spinach, mix well then transfer to a large mixing bowl.

Beat the egg whites to stiff peaks and fold into the spinach mixture. Spoon into the ramekins, filling them level. Set the dishes in a large roasting tin. Add boiling water from the kettle to a depth of about 2.5 cm (1 in). Bake for 20 minutes or until the soufflés are well risen. Remove the ramekins from the tin, cool for 10 minutes, then loosen the sides and turn out into a buttered gratin dish – right sides up. The soufflés can be set aside overnight.

If the soufflés have been chilled, allow them at least 1 hour to return to room temperature. Heat the oven to 200°C/400°F/Gas Mark 6. Pour the cream over the soufflés, coating each one. Sprinkle with Parmesan and place the dish in the oven for 15 minutes or until the sauce is bubbling, then serve.

Honey-glazed duck in grapefruit and ginger sauce

Roast duck goes well with anything tangy; my choice is grapefruit,
with fruit segments served in a sauce made with fresh ginger.

*10 Gressingham duck breast
 fillets
1 tablespoon clear honey
1 tablespoon dark soy sauce*

For the sauce

*4 grapefruit
75 g (3 oz) granulated sugar
400 ml (14 fl oz) fresh
 grapefruit juice
3 tablespoons clear honey
2 tablespoons dark soy sauce
Juice 1 lemon
2.5 cm (1 in) grated fresh
 ginger
3 tablespoons cornflour*

Prick the skin on each duck breast fillet with a fork. Blend the
honey and soy sauce to make a glaze and brush over the fillets.
Set them skin-side-up on a rack in a roasting tin. Refrigerate until
ready to cook.

To make the sauce, slice away the outer peel and white pith
from the grapefruit. With a sharp knife, cut into the fruits between
the membrane to lift out the segments. Reserve the fruit and any
juice in a bowl. Put the sugar into a dry pan. Set over a moderate
heat and stir until the sugar melts and turns to caramel. Draw off
the heat and add the fruit juice – cover your hand as the mixture
will boil up furiously with the addition of cold liquid. Replace the
pan over the heat – if there are any lumps of caramel, stir over a
low heat until they dissolve. Add the honey, soy sauce, lemon juice
and ginger. Stir until the mixture simmers. Blend the cornflour
with 2 tablespoons of cold water. Stir into the pan and cook,
stirring until the sauce thickens and clears. Remove from the heat.

Heat the oven to 200°C/400°F/Gas Mark 6. Set the duck
fillets in the oven and roast for 35–40 minutes until the skins are
golden and the flesh is still a little pink. Reheat the sauce, add
the grapefruit pieces and any juices in the bowl. Slice each fillet
lengthways into three, arrange on a heated platter and spoon over
the grapefruit and ginger sauce.

Pot-roasted new potatoes

Here's a great no-fuss method of cooking new potatoes – in their own steam. You will also need some sea salt flakes.

1.5 kg (3 lb) new potatoes or
  a waxy salad variety
4 tablespoons olive oil
Sea salt flakes and freshly
  milled pepper

Rinse the potatoes – there's no need to scrub or scrape them. Leave small ones whole and slice larger ones in half lengthways. Place the potatoes in a roomy casserole; they should no more than half fill the container – use two containers if necessary. Add the olive oil and turn the potatoes to coat them with it. Cover with the casserole lid.

Heat the oven to 190°C/375°F/Gas Mark 5. Set the covered casserole in the heated oven and cook for 40–60 minutes or until the potatoes are tender when pierced with a knife tip. Sprinkle with sea salt and milled pepper, toss and serve.

French-style peas

This is a brilliant way to add extra interest to fresh or frozen peas.

1 Cos lettuce
2 bunches spring onions
50 g (2 oz) butter
900 g (2 lb) shelled fresh or
  frozen peas
1 teaspoon caster sugar
Salt and freshly milled black
  pepper
2–3 tablespoons chopped
  parsley or chervil

Remove the coarse outer leaves from the lettuce, then cut the firm heart into chunky pieces. Trim the root and green stems from the spring onions, leaving the bulbs whole.

Melt 40 g (1½ oz) of the butter in a pan. Add the lettuce, onions, peas, sugar, seasoning and 3 tablespoons of cold water. Cover with the pan lid – it should fit tightly – and place over a medium heat. After 2–3 minutes reduce the heat to the lowest setting and cook for 20 minutes – shake the pan occasionally but don't remove the lid. Check the seasoning, stir in the remaining butter and the herbs, and serve.

Chocolate rum cake

To turn a cake into a dessert, simply soak it in a flavoured syrup. The cake takes up the flavour and becomes soft and crumbly – just add whipped cream and a pretty fruit sauce.

200 g (7 oz) plain flour
25 g (1 oz) cocoa
2 teaspoons baking powder
½ teaspoon salt
200 g (7 oz) light muscovado sugar
100 ml (3½ fl oz) sunflower oil
150 ml (5 fl oz) milk
3 eggs
½ teaspoon vanilla essence

For the syrup and topping
100 g (4 oz) granulated sugar
6 tablespoons dark rum

For the topping
400 ml (14 fl oz) double cream
Cocoa for dusting

Heat the oven to 160°C/325°F/Gas Mark 3. Butter and base line one 23 cm (9 in) round cake tin or spring-form tin. Sift the flour, cocoa, baking powder, salt and muscovado sugar into a mixing bowl.

In a measuring jug, combine the sunflower oil and milk. Separate the eggs, reserving the whites and adding the yolks to the liquid ingredients. Mix the egg yolks, vanilla, milk and oil with a fork. Add the liquid to the dry ingredients and mix with a wooden spoon to a smooth, slack batter. Beat the egg whites to stiff peaks and fold into the cake batter. Pour the mixture into the prepared tin. Set in the heated oven and bake for 45 minutes – test with a cake skewer.

Meanwhile measure the sugar for the syrup and 200 ml (7 fl oz) cold water into a pan and set over a low heat until the sugar dissolves. Bring to the boil and draw off the heat. Add the rum. Prick the surface of the hot cake with a fork, and spoon the syrup over it. Leave in the baking tin until completely cold. Turn the cake layer out, peel off the baking paper, and set on a serving platter. Whip the cream to soft peaks and swirl over the top of the cake layer. Chill until firm – at least 2 hours. Then dust with cocoa and serve slices with the red fruit sauce.

Katie's tip
When cutting a fragile party cake, the trick is to use a hot wet knife – this way you avoid dragging crumbs from one slice to the next. Dip a kitchen knife into a jug of hot water, shake off the water and cut. Wipe the blade clean, and repeat for each slice. Sounds like a lot of trouble but it's worth it for the smart appearance.

Red fruit sauce

This makes a great topping for vanilla ice-cream too.

500 g (1 lb 2 oz) fresh or
*   frozen raspberries*
5 tablespoons redcurrant jelly
2 tablespoons cornflour
Juice 1 lemon
500 g (1 lb 2 oz) fresh
*   strawberries*

Put the raspberries in a pan, add the jelly and stir over a low heat until the fruits are softened, the juices run and the jelly has melted. Blend the cornflour with 2 tablespoons of cold water until smooth and add to the fruit mixture. Stir until the mixture has thickened and boiled, then remove from the heat. Sieve and discard the raspberry pips. Add the lemon juice and let the sauce cool. To serve, add the strawberries sliced lengthways in quarters.

 Wine recommendations

Serve a creamy-rich sparkling wine from either Australia or South Africa, preferably one with a good proportion of Chardonnay in it, to kick off this celebratory spread. Your guests can enjoy an apéritif glass while you hand round the canapés, and you'll find it will go perfectly with the feather-light spinach soufflés. The honey-glazed duck needs a big fruit-filled red with the softness of oak-ageing to match the richness of the meat and the fruitiness of the sauce. This is Australian Shiraz territory *par excellence*, but you could also consider a sweetly spicy Zinfandel from California. Oak-aged American Merlot would work well too. The chocolate rum cake would be best served by a contrastingly light dessert wine. Try Italian Moscato d'Asti from Piedmont, the less fizzy cousin of Asti itself.

Supper at the kitchen table

Serve yourself supper

Easy-going entertaining

Summertime spread

Casual Suppers

SUPPER AT THE KITCHEN TABLE

menu for 6

- SMOKED HADDOCK PÂTÉ
- CORN-FED CHICKEN WITH LEMON AND SHALLOTS
- GARLIC AND OLIVE OIL MASH
- GLAZED CARROTS
- COFFEE WALNUT PUDDINGS WITH COFFEE CREAM SAUCE

This is an informal menu that concentrates on easily managed and quickly prepared comfort food – we all love it! A smoked haddock pâté takes only moments to buzz in the blender and it has a superb flavour. Make sure it's well chilled, then serve with slices of unbuttered hot toast or with crisp Melba toast.

What could be more delicious for a main course than a tangy chicken casserole, cooked with an unthickened gravy flavoured with lemon, herbs and a hint of cinnamon? An outdoor-reared or corn-fed chicken will have an excellent flavour and it takes only an extra few minutes to joint a whole bird into pieces. If you're happier making the whole dish in advance,

it reheats very well. Serve with a flavoured potato mash to mop up the chicken juices (if garlic isn't for you, stir in a couple of tablespoons of grated Parmesan instead). Prepare your potato mash with care: the cooked potatoes must be pressed through a sieve, seasoned and enriched with butter and cream – they will taste delicious. Add glazed carrots, oven-cooked with the addition of brown sugar to emphasize their natural sweetness, and you have comfort food at its best.

A hot pudding is always welcome, and I guarantee your guests will love these individual coffee walnut puddings – in my opinion, they're even better than sticky toffee puddings!

timeplan

The day before

Make smoked haddock pâté and refrigerate. Prepare Melba toast. Cook corn-fed chicken with lemon and sweet shallots – cool and refrigerate.

In the morning

Prepare coffee walnut puddings. Combine ingredients for sauce and refrigerate.

1 hour before

Remove smoked haddock pâté from refrigerator.

40 minutes before

Reheat chicken. Make garlic and olive oil mashed potatoes. Cook carrots.

Last minute

Put coffee walnut puddings in oven to steam.

Smoked haddock pâté

Serve the pâté with Melba toast or slices of toasted wholemeal bread.

450 g (1 lb) smoked haddock
  fillet
100 g (4 oz) butter
250 g (9 oz) curd cheese
Freshly milled pepper
1 tablespoon lemon juice

To serve

Lemon slice and fresh bay leaf
8 slices bread

Cut the haddock into 4 pieces. Melt 75 g (3 oz) of the butter in a large pan over a low heat, add the pieces of fish and cover with the lid. Don't add any water – just allow the fish to stew gently in the butter until tender, about 5 minutes. Let the fish cool in the pan, then lift away the skin and coarsely flake the flesh.

Turn the flaked haddock and the buttery juices from the pan into the bowl of a food processor. Add the curd cheese, milled pepper and lemon juice and blend to a purée. Spoon the mixture into a serving dish. Melt the remaining butter and spoon over. Decorate with a lemon slice and a bay leaf. Chill the pâté for 4 hours or overnight. Serve with toasted wholemeal bread or slices of Melba toast.

To make Melba toast, take 8 medium-cut slices from a large white or a malted brown loaf. Toast the bread slices on both sides. While hot, trim the crusts, then cut each slice in half horizontally, through the middle, to leave 16 thin slices. Cut each slice diagonally into triangles and brown the untoasted sides under a grill – they will curl up at the edges and become crisp. Serve at once or store in a tightly closed plastic bag.

Corn-fed chicken with lemon and shallots

You can't always buy corn-fed chicken in portions so it's well worth knowing how to cut up a whole bird yourself.

6 chicken breast fillets or
*   2 x 1.25 kg (2½–3 lb)*
*   corn-fed chickens*
4 tablespoons olive oil
Grated rind and juice
*   2 lemons*
450 g (1 lb) shallots
25 g (1 oz) butter
1 cinnamon stick
1 tablespoon Dijon mustard
2 tablespoons clear honey
1 teaspoon dried oregano or
*   1 tablespoon oregano,*
*   freshly chopped*
300 ml (10 fl oz) chicken or
*   vegetable stock*
Salt and freshly milled pepper
100 ml (3½ fl oz) dry white
*   wine*

If you have chosen to cook fillets, cut each one in half diagonally. For the whole birds, remove any trussing string and place the first bird on a cutting board with the breast upwards. Cut off the legs, then cut each leg at the joint into drumstick and thigh. Take the knife along either side of the breast bone and remove the breasts and wings together. Cut off the wing tips. Slice each breast in half on the diagonal. You'll have 8 pieces. Repeat with the second bird.

Measure the olive oil into a shallow dish and mix in the finely grated lemon rind. Turn the pieces of chicken in the oil and lemon mixture and leave to marinate for up to 2 hours. Peel the shallots and leave them whole.

Heat the oven to 190°C/375°F/Gas Mark 5. Set a dry frying-pan over a moderate heat until hot. Add the chicken pieces, skin side down, and let them sizzle until they are golden brown; turn over for a moment to seal. Do this in batches, transferring the chicken pieces from the pan to a casserole or large oven dish. Pour off the chicken drippings. Add the butter to the hot pan and then the shallots. Stir the shallots over a moderate heat until they begin to colour and caramelize around the edges. Drain, then add to the chicken with the cinnamon stick.

In a bowl combine the lemon juice, mustard, honey and oregano. Stir in the stock and a seasoning of salt and milled pepper. Pour this over the chicken and add the wine – the liquid should barely cover the chicken pieces. Cover with the casserole lid, or enclose an oven dish with kitchen foil, set in the heated oven and cook for 1 hour until the chicken is tender and no pink juices run when it is pierced with a knife tip. Spoon the chicken, sweet shallots and gravy on to a warmed platter and serve.

Katie's tip

It's worth remembering that dry white vermouth, which has a delicious herby flavour, is a good substitute for white wine in a recipe. It needs to be diluted with an equal part of cold water. At other times, try adding a splash of vermouth to the poaching syrup for dried fruits and taste the difference.

Garlic and olive oil mash

For a creamy consistency always mash potatoes when they're hot and newly cooked. Never whiz in a food processor as they go gluey. Use a mouli-légume or a potato ricer for a perfect purée.

1 kg (2¼ lb) potatoes
4 cloves garlic
1 teaspoon salt
150 ml (5 fl oz) single cream
3 tablespoons olive oil or
* melted butter*
Freshly milled pepper
Olive oil and flatleaf parsley,
* to serve*

Peel the potatoes and cut into even-sized pieces. Cover with cold water, bring to a simmer and cook for 15–20 minutes until tender. Peel the garlic cloves and mash to a purée with salt. Set the cream to warm in a separate pan.

When the potatoes are tender, drain them well. Return the potatoes to the hot pan and shake over the heat for a moment to dry off and become floury. Press (don't rub or stir) the potatoes through a sieve into a warmed mixing bowl. Beat in the olive oil or melted butter and then the warmed cream, gradually, until you have a piping hot and fluffy, but creamy, potato purée the consistency you like. Beat in the mashed garlic, salt and a good seasoning of milled pepper. Taste and check the seasoning and flavour. The mash will probably have to be kept hot, so cover with a plate and stand the bowl over a pan of simmering water until serving time.

Stir the potato and pile into a warm serving dish. Top with an extra drizzle of olive oil and a scattering of coarsely snipped, flatleaf parsley.

Glazed carrots

For the final stage of cooking this accompaniment, slide the carrots into the oven under the chicken, if you like.

900 g (2 lb) carrots
50 g (2 oz) light muscovado
* sugar*
25 g (1 oz) butter
Salt and freshly milled pepper
½ teaspoon cracked pepper

Heat the oven to 180°C/350°F/Gas Mark 4. Trim the carrots, pare and then cut lengthways and across in chunky sticks. Cover the carrots with cold water and bring to a simmer; cook for 10 minutes, then drain. Arrange the hot carrots in a buttered casserole or baking dish, in layers with the brown sugar, the butter in flakes and a seasoning of salt and freshly milled pepper.

Nearer serving time, add 2 tablespoons of cold water to the carrots. Cover with the casserole lid (use kitchen foil over a baking dish) and bake in the heated oven for 20–30 minutes. Turn the contents of the casserole into a warmed serving dish, sprinkle with cracked pepper (sometimes called steak pepper) and serve.

Coffee walnut puddings with coffee cream sauce

Make sure the butter is at room temperature; it will blend better.

For the walnut topping

50 g (2 oz) butter
*75 g (3 oz) light muscovado
    sugar*
50 g (2 oz) broken walnuts

For the cake mixture

*1 tablespoon instant coffee
    granules*
150 g (5 oz) self-raising flour
1 teaspoon baking powder
*50 g (2 oz) light muscovado
    sugar*
*1 rounded tablespoon golden
    syrup*
100 g (4 oz) soft butter
2 eggs

For the coffee cream sauce

*1 tablespoon instant coffee
    granules*
*2 tablespoons light muscovado
    sugar*
*300 ml (10 fl oz) double
    cream*

Melt the butter for the walnut topping and use a little to brush around the insides of six 150 ml (5 fl oz) pudding moulds. To the remaining melted butter, add the sugar and 1 tablespoon of cold water. Warm to dissolve the sugar, then stir in the broken walnuts. Spoon the walnut topping equally into each mould and chill.

Combine the coffee granules with 2 tablespoons of boiling water, stir to make a strong coffee liquid and allow to cool. Sift the flour and baking powder into a medium-sized mixing bowl and add the sugar, golden syrup, soft butter, eggs and the liquid coffee. Mix with a wooden spoon, or use an electric hand whisk, to form a smooth cake mixture. Spoon this mixture into each pudding mould to about two-thirds full. Cover each pudding with a square of buttered kitchen foil, pressing it around the sides of the moulds. At this stage you can set the puddings aside until cooking time. If chilled, bring them out 30 minutes before, to regain room temperature.

Heat the oven to 190°C/375°F/Gas Mark 5. Put the covered puddings in a roasting tin so they don't touch and pour in boiling water to a depth of about 2.5 cm (1 in). Cut a piece of kitchen foil large enough to completely cover the tin and puddings. Place over the top and tuck under the edge of the roasting tin. Set in the oven and 'oven steam' for 40 minutes. Once cooked, these puddings will keep hot for up to 30 minutes. Leave in the hot water in the covered tin.

For the sauce, warm the coffee granules, sugar and cream in a small pan – do not boil. Remove the foil from the roasting tin and each pudding. Turn the puddings on to warmed serving plates. Drizzle over the coffee cream sauce or serve separately.

Wine recommendations

The smokiness of the fish in the pâté calls for a similarly smoky, i.e. oak-matured, wine to be served with it, but go for something with a little more acid grip than most Chardonnay has. Oaky dry white Bordeaux, a blend of Sémillon and Sauvignon Blanc, would be a canny choice, as might a lightly oaked Spanish or Italian white. With the chicken, a soft, supple red will work best in the context of this menu. Think Pinot Noir or Merlot from Chile or California, or perhaps one of the more upmarket Reserve Merlots from eastern Europe. Then break with convention, and try a small tot of one of the sweet, dark fortified wines with the coffee puddings, perhaps a Marsala Dolce or a Malmsey Madeira.

SERVE YOURSELF SUPPER

menu for 8

- SMOKED FISH CANAPÉS
- MARINATED CHICKEN IN A LEMON AND TARRAGON DRESSING
- STIR-FRIED VEGETABLE SALAD
- NEW POTATO SALAD
- FRESH APRICOT TART

For laid-back entertaining, here's a relaxed fork supper designed around dishes that can be prepared ahead and then served with a minimum of fuss – just add finishing touches so that it all looks absolutely fresh. I suggest that you start with some tempting smoked fish canapés on brown soda bread slices to pass around with drinks. The close texture of this traditional bread provides the perfect platform for the intense flavour of smoked fish partnered variously with horseradish, soy, mustard and ginger for extra interest and 'bite'.

Set out your table with a pretty platter of cold chicken, tender breast meat marinated in an oil and

The day before
Prepare chicken and marinate in dressing. Bake apricot tart. Make potato salad and chill.

In the morning
Prepare smoked fish canapés, assemble on serving plates and cover with cling film. Prepare and stir-fry vegetables.

1–2 hours before
Add watercress to stir-fried vegetable salad and toss. Turn marinated chicken on to serving platter and add garnish. Remove potato salad from the refrigerator.

Last minute
Dust apricot tart with icing sugar.

vinegar dressing, strongly flavoured with lemon and tarragon, to make a change from the more often used mayonnaise dressings.

With this main dish, serve a new potato salad, which is always popular, and a stir-fried vegetable salad with appealing colours and textures and a hint of sesame oil in the seasoning. Toasted cashew nuts and coriander give an oriental flavour.

As a final flourish, produce an apricot tart – apricot preserve, baked almond filling and fresh ripe apricots in a pastry shell – dusted with icing sugar and served with pouring cream. It couldn't be easier.

Smoked fish canapés

These are so good that you'll need at least three per guest. Traditional brown soda bread provides a firm, flavoursome base.

4 tablespoons olive oil
1 tablespoon soy sauce
1 tablespoon brown sugar
2 peppered smoked mackerel
   fillets, coarsely flaked
200 g (7 oz) smoked
   haddock, filleted and cut
   into thin slivers
Juice 1 lemon
150 g (5 oz) sliced smoked
   salmon
200 g (7 oz) smoked cod's
   roe
200 g (7 oz) crème fraîche
Horseradish relish and Dijon
   mustard
2 tablespoons caster sugar
2 tablespoons white wine
   vinegar
Coarse black pepper for
   seasoning
2–3 pieces stem ginger in
   syrup, cut into slivers
2–3 shallots, sliced into rings
1 large cucumber, sliced,
   lightly salted and allowed to
   wilt, then rinsed and
   pressed dry
400 g (14 oz) brown soda
   bread loaf, thinly sliced
Unsalted butter for spreading
Chopped fresh dill and chives

Combine the oil, soy sauce and brown sugar to make a dressing. Toss the mackerel in it and set aside. Put the haddock and lemon juice in a bowl and leave to marinate. Cut the salmon into slivers – two pieces per canapé – and scoop the cod's roe from the skin.

Flavour half the crème fraîche (2 tablespoons) with 1 teaspoon of horseradish relish and half with 1 teaspoon of Dijon mustard.

Prepare the pickling mixture: combine the caster sugar with 2 tablespoons of boiling water, stir to dissolve, then add the vinegar and season with pepper. Pour into three tiny bowls and in each place separately the stem ginger, shallot rings and cucumber slices. Marinate until assembly time, then drain.

To assemble, lightly butter the slices of soda bread and cut each into 3/4 pieces. Divide the bread pieces equally into 4 batches and top each with these combinations:
1) slivers of salmon, topped by horseradish-flavoured crème fraîche and dill; 2) 1 teaspoon of cod's roe, pickled shallot rings, pepper and chives; 3) mackerel flakes and pickled cucumber slices; and 4) slivers of smoked haddock, mustard-flavoured crème fraîche and pickled ginger. Arrange on serving platters and cover with cling film. They will stay fresh for several hours.

Marinated chicken in a lemon and tarragon dressing

Chicken breast is deliciously tender and quite filling – six good-sized breasts are plenty for eight servings.

6 chicken breasts, with skin on
1 tablespoon olive oil
175 ml (6 fl oz) vegetable
*   stock*

For the dressing

Grated rind and juice 1 lemon
1 tablespoon white wine
*   vinegar*
1 garlic clove, peeled and
*   crushed*
1 teaspoon Dijon mustard
1 tablespoon soft brown sugar
175 ml (6 fl oz) olive oil
Salt and freshly milled pepper
2 tablespoons chopped fresh
*   tarragon*

For the decoration

100 g (4 oz) green olives
Fresh tarragon leaves
Grated lemon rind

Preheat the oven to 180°C/350°F/Gas Mark 4. Arrange the chicken breasts, skin-side-up, in a deep, ovenproof dish that is not too large, so that they remain closely packed. Brush the skins with olive oil. Pour in enough vegetable stock to cover partially but not submerge them. Bake in the oven for 30–35 minutes, then remove and allow to cool in the stock before refrigerating.

To make the dressing: combine the lemon rind and juice with the vinegar then add the garlic, mustard, sugar and oil. Season, mix well and then add the chopped tarragon leaves.

Lift the chicken breasts from the stock and remove the skins. Slice the meat diagonally, or tear into strips with a fork. Place the pieces in a bowl, pour over the dressing and marinate in the refrigerator until serving time. To serve, arrange the chicken pieces in a shallow serving dish and scatter with olives, tarragon leaves and grated lemon rind.

Stir-fried vegetable salad

The best way to tackle this unusual salad is to stir-fry each vegetable separately, then dress with sesame oil, lemon juice and seasoning.

4 tablespoons grapeseed oil, or any light cooking oil
100 g (4 oz) cashew nuts
2.5 cm (1 in) fresh ginger, peeled, thinly sliced and cut into fine matchstick-sized strips
200 g (7 oz) thin green beans, trimmed but with the tails left on
2 yellow sweet peppers, halved, deseeded and cut into thin strips
1 bunch spring onions, trimmed and sliced diagonally
200 g (7 oz) asparagus tips, trimmed into 5 cm (2 in) lengths
1–2 tablespoons chopped fresh coriander
1 teaspoon sesame oil
Juice 1 lemon
Salt and freshly milled black pepper
85 g pack watercress

Heat 1 tablespoon of oil in a wok or a 25 cm (10 in) frying-pan. When hot, stir-fry the cashew nuts until golden. Remove from the pan and set aside. Add a further 1 tablespoon of oil, then stir-fry ginger for ½ minute. Add the beans and continue cooking for 4–5 minutes, until tender but still crunchy. Transfer to a large bowl. Add another tablespoon of oil and stir-fry peppers for 2–3 minutes, adding the spring onions at the last moment. Add the peppers and onions to the beans.

Finally, add 1 tablespoon of oil and stir-fry the asparagus tips for 3–4 minutes. Add 2–3 tablespoons of water, cover the pan and steam for about 5 minutes until tender (test by biting into a stalk). Add the asparagus to the other vegetables along with the cashew nuts, coriander, sesame oil and lemon juice. Season to taste. Toss together and set aside to cool.

Just before serving, twist off the watercress stalks and add the leaves to the salad. Toss again and transfer to a serving bowl.

Katie's tip

Onions are often too pungent to use raw in summer salads or sandwiches. You can always choose a mild variety, like the sweeter red onions; shallots would work well, too. Alternatively, you can change the nature of an onion by blanching it. Place the onion slices in a bowl, cover with boiling water, stand for 5 minutes, then drain and chill. They will now taste quite mild. I like to use onion rings prepared this way, then tossed with soured cream and seasoning, as a relish.

New potato salad

I prefer medium-sized new potatoes, sliced thickly. For the best potato salad ever, add the olive oil and vinegar dressing when the potatoes are hot and the mayonnaise when cold.

900 g (2 lb) new potatoes
3 tablespoons olive oil
1 tablespoon white wine vinegar
Salt and freshly milled black
  pepper
1 tablespoon finely chopped
  red onion
2 tablespoons snipped chives
2 tablespoons mayonnaise
2 tablespoons natural yoghurt
1 teaspoon Dijon mustard

Rinse the potatoes and boil in their skins until just tender. Drain, then turn on to a clean tea towel to dry. When they're cool enough to handle, peel off their skins and slice thickly.

To make the dressing: combine the oil and vinegar and season. Add the onion and chives. Gently stir the dressing into the potatoes and marinate for at least 1 hour.

Blend the mayonnaise with the yoghurt and mustard. Add to the cold potato salad and carefully mix in, then turn into a serving bowl. This salad will keep for at least 24 hours in the refrigerator and even seems to improve in flavour.

Fresh apricot tart

I love the flavour of this tart. The icing sugar dissolves over the cut apricots but remains on the baked almond filling in attractive contrast.

Shortcrust pastry, made with
* 75 g (3 oz) butter and*
* 175 g (6 oz) flour*

For the filling
75 g (3 oz) butter
75 g (3 oz) caster sugar
2 eggs
100 g (4 oz) ground almonds
1 teaspoon vanilla essence
2 tablespoons apricot preserve
700 g (1½ lb) fresh apricots,
* halved, stones removed*
2 tablespoons flaked almonds
Icing sugar for dusting
Cream for pouring

Preheat the oven to 190°C/375°F/Gas Mark 5 and put a baking tray in the oven. Line a 23 cm (9 in) tart tin (preferably with a loose base) with shortcrust pastry. Chill in the refrigerator while you make the filling.

Cream the butter and sugar in a bowl until soft and light. Add the eggs, ground almonds and vanilla essence and mix to a soft, smooth paste. Spread the apricot preserve over the pastry base. Spoon on the almond mixture and spread it out level. Arrange apricot halves close together on top, cut sides up. Scatter with flaked almonds.

Place the tart directly on to the hot tray in the oven and bake for 15 minutes. Lower the temperature to 180°C/350°F/Gas Mark 4 and bake for 40 minutes, or until the almond mixture has set and the pastry is golden. Leave to cool, then dust with icing sugar. Serve cut into slices with cream to pour over.

Wine recommendations

A freshly opened, and vigorously chilled, bottle of pale dry sherry – fino or manzanilla – will not only act as a highly efficient apéritif, but will also beautifully complement the smoked fish appetizers. If you prefer something with a slightly lower alcohol content, then choose a crisp Sauvignon or Chenin Blanc white from the Loire Valley. With the cold chicken, opt for a dry white with a little more substance. Wines made from the fashionable Viognier grape, from southern France, Argentina or Chile, would nicely match the aniseedy tang of the tarragon in the recipe. The apricot tart needs a late-harvested dessert wine, a Muscat or Riesling from California or Washington State or a German Riesling of the Auslese category.

EASY-GOING ENTERTAINING

menu for 6

- CUCUMBER AND MINT DIP
- ROASTED AUBERGINE DIP
- CIABATTA BREAD TOAST
- FRESH SPAGHETTI WITH CHILLI SAUCE AND TIGER PRAWNS
- GREEN LEAF AND CITRUS SALAD
- LEMON TART

This supper menu is peppered with zesty flavours to cheer up a chilly winter evening. The choice of dishes here will be a talking point so invite friends who like something innovative and new. There are two Mediterranean recipes to start with: a cucumber and mint dip and a roasted aubergine dip, to be scooped up with slices of hot, toasted ciabatta bread. Pour some wine and encourage your guests to dip in – they will be pleasantly occupied while you get on with the last-minute cooking of the main course.

Pasta is a very sociable food and what could be nicer than sharing with friends a big bowl of chilli-flavoured spaghetti and delicious tiger prawns, sprinkled with Parmesan? I use the red jalapeño chillies you find sold loose in any supermarket, which are medium hot. The

timeplan

The day before

Prepare and bake lemon tart. Make both cucumber and mint and roasted aubergine dips and chill. Make chilli sauce for the spaghetti.

Early in the morning

Prepare salad leaves and chill in closed bag; cut orange segments and make up citrus vinaigrette.

Last minute

Toast ciabatta bread and cut slices. Mix and toss salad. Cook spaghetti, toss with chilli sauce; fry prawns and add. Warm lemon tart.

sauce is unusual because it's not really a sauce as you would expect; rather it is a concentrate of chillies and tomatoes with an olive oil base that coats the strands of pasta. The flavours are superb. To serve afterwards, a green leaf and citrus fruit salad is cool and fresh-tasting. I don't like piling too many different flavour combinations on my plate, and in this case the idea of having salad as a separate course works better.

I have yet to meet a lemon tart that tastes better than this recipe of mine. It's sharp and clean and, as if that's not enough, it's just so easy to make. Before baking make sure that the oven shelf is in the right position and level, as this tart is very full. Before taking it to the table, briefly warm the tart through to crisp up the pastry – utterly delicious!

Cucumber and mint dip

Be sure to use thick Greek-style yoghurt for this subtle-flavoured dip.

½ cucumber
1 x 500 g tub thick Greek-style yoghurt
1 clove garlic, peeled and lightly crushed
2 tablespoons extra virgin olive oil
2 teaspoons white wine vinegar
Salt and freshly milled pepper
1–2 tablespoons chopped fresh mint or 1 teaspoon dried mint

Peel the cucumber, cut it in half lengthways and scoop out the seeds with a teaspoon. Cut the cucumber lengthways into thin strips and across into fine dice.

Turn the yoghurt into a bowl. Add the crushed garlic, diced cucumber, 1 tablespoon of the olive oil, wine vinegar, a seasoning of salt and freshly milled pepper and the mint. Stir to blend. Cover and refrigerate for at least 1 hour so that the flavours can develop. Stir and turn into a serving bowl. Drizzle with remaining olive oil and serve.

Roasted aubergine dip

Don't be tempted to make a smaller quantity as the aubergines reduce once they have been baked and their juices squeezed out.

900 g (2 lb) aubergines
2 cloves garlic
Juice 1 lemon
75 ml (3 fl oz) olive oil
Salt and freshly milled pepper
50 g (2 oz) black olives, stoned and chopped

Heat the oven to 200°C/400°F/Gas Mark 6. Stab the aubergines all over with a knife point and place on a baking tray. Set in the heated oven and roast for 40–45 minutes, turning them over once about halfway through. To check if they are cooked, poke with a small sharp knife – if they feel soft all the way through, have collapsed slightly and are wrinkled, they are ready. Remove the aubergines from the oven and allow them to cool. Then cut off the stems, peel away the skin and discard both.

Over a bowl, firmly squeeze the peeled aubergines to remove as much of their juices as possible. Place the squeezed aubergine flesh in a food-processor bowl. Add the crushed garlic and the lemon juice. Whiz to a purée and then, with the blades running, slowly pour the olive oil into the mixture. Switch off the food processor, and season the dip to taste with salt and milled pepper. Transfer to a serving dish. Pile the chopped olives in the middle of the dip and serve.

Ciabatta bread toast

Slice 1–2 ciabatta loaves in half horizontally – this way you get the pretty texture of the inside of the loaf. Slide the bread halves, cut-sides-up, under a heated grill and toast until golden. Now cut across each bread slice in thick fingers and serve warm, alongside the dips.

Fresh spaghetti with chilli sauce and tiger prawns

Chilli may seem an unusual partner for pasta, but it makes a really wonderful combination that's just bursting with flavour – the prawns turn this into an extra special dish.

2 red jalapeño chillies
3 cloves garlic
Salt
100 ml (3½ fl oz) olive oil
6 sun-dried tomatoes in oil
500 g (1 lb 2 oz) fresh
*   raw tiger prawns or*
*   2 x 200 g packs frozen raw*
*   tiger-prawn tails, thawed*
700 g (1½ lb) fresh spaghetti
50g (2 oz) butter
Freshly milled pepper
50g (2 oz) grated Parmesan,
*   to serve*

Seed and coarsely chop the chillies. Peel and mash the garlic with a good pinch of salt. Put the chillies and mashed garlic in a food processor and whiz to chop finely. With the motor running, slowly pour in the olive oil. Still with the motor running, drop in the sun-dried tomatoes (drained from the oil in the jar) and you will finish up with a thick chilli sauce.

Peel the shells from the raw tiger prawns. Add the fresh spaghetti to one or two large pans of boiling salted water (you will need approximately 6 litres (10½ pints) of water and 2–3 table-spoons of salt), stir as the water reboils and cook the pasta for 3–4 minutes, then drain. While the pasta is simmering, melt the butter in a frying-pan, add the tiger prawns and stir until they are cooked – they will turn pink.

Turn the drained spaghetti into a hot serving bowl, season with freshly milled pepper, add the chilli sauce and toss to mix through – the chilli sauce should coat the spaghetti strands.

Add the prawns and buttery juices from the pan and toss again before serving. Serve with plenty of grated Parmesan.

Katie's tip

Fresh pasta is not necessarily better than dried. A low-grade fresh pasta made using mixed flours is easily over-cooked, becoming soft and sticky – it's always advisable to tease out or shake loose coils of fresh pasta before adding to the cooking pot. Unless you can source freshly made pasta from a good retailer, when it will be delicious, you are just as well off with a quality dried pasta. Look for pasta made with hard durum-wheat semolina. Fresh pasta will cook more quickly – when it rises to the surface of the cooking water it's ready. Follow cooking directions on the packet for dried pasta. Use plenty of well-salted water in two pans if you don't have a really large pasta pan.

Green leaf and citrus salad

Oranges are a lovely fruit for adding to salad; they are cool and fresh-tasting and they look pretty, too – making this the perfect dish to follow a warming chilli-flavoured pasta.

1 Iceberg lettuce
1 cucumber
1 bunch spring onions
3 tablespoons chopped parsley
4 oranges

For the citrus vinaigrette

1 teaspoon grated orange rind
3 tablespoons orange juice
2 tablespoons wine vinegar
1 tablespoon clear honey
Salt and freshly milled pepper
75–100 ml (3–3½ fl oz)
   olive oil

With a kitchen knife cut the lettuce into quarters, then cut across the quarter sections to chop the leaves coarsely, and pile them into a large salad bowl. Slice the cucumber thinly. Trim the spring onions, then chop all the white and some green stems. Add the cucumber, spring onions and chopped parsley to the bowl.

Take a slice from the top and base of each orange and cut round and round (like an apple) to remove the outer peel and white pith. Holding each orange in turn over a bowl, cut into the fruit and lift out the orange sections. Combine the ingredients for the orange vinaigrette and taste for seasoning.

When ready to serve, add the orange segments and prepared dressing to the salad bowl and toss to mix.

Lemon tart

If you find it tricky transferring a tart like this with liquid contents, take the lemon filling in a jug to the oven and fill the tart on the spot before sliding it on to the shelf for baking.

Shortcrust pastry, made with
75 g (3 oz) butter and
175 g (6 oz) flour

For the filling
4 eggs
225g (8 oz) caster sugar
Finely grated rind and juice
of 3 lemons
75g (3 oz) butter
Icing sugar, to decorate

Heat the oven to 190°C/375°F/Gas Mark 5. Place a baking tray in the oven as it heats up. Roll the prepared pastry on a floured work surface to a circle large enough to line a 23 cm (9 in) tart tin, preferably with a loose bottom. Line the tart tin, trim excess pastry and put tart to chill for 20 minutes. Put a circle of greaseproof paper and a few baking beans in the unbaked tart to weight down the pastry. Place the lined tart tin directly on to the hot baking tray and bake for 12 minutes to set the pastry. Remove from the oven, and discard the lining paper and baking beans. Lower the oven heat to 180°C/350°F/Gas Mark 4.

Combine the eggs, sugar, lemon rind and butter in a medium mixing bowl. Set the bowl over a pan quarter-filled with hot water. Stir until the sugar has dissolved and the butter melted. Stir in the lemon juice. Pour the mixture into the pie shell (still on the baking tray). Return the baking tray with the tart to the oven and bake for 20 minutes or until the filling has set. Cool for 5 minutes, then lift the tart from the baking tray and slide on to a wire cooling rack.

Serve this lemon tart warm – if baked ahead, slide back on to the baking tray and pop into a moderate oven (180°C/350°F/Gas Mark 4) for 5–8 minutes, then dust generously with icing sugar.

 Wine recommendations

A zesty dry white with refreshing levels of acidity and plenty of fruit will work best with the dips. Dry Rieslings made in the steely modern style are a surefire bet, whether from Australia, Alsace or New Zealand. For the spaghetti dish, you'll need something a little weightier and rounder, and with a touch of spice in the flavour to enable it to hold its own against the chilli in the sauce. Pinot Gris or Viognier are grape varieties to consider, or try a delicately oaked white Bordeaux with plenty of Sémillon. With the lemon tart, a late-picked Riesling or Muscat from Australia or California, or perhaps a Vendange Tardive wine from either of those grape varieties from Alsace, would all suit.

SUMMERTIME SPREAD

menu for 8

- ASPARAGUS WITH CHOPPED EGGS
- MEDITERRANEAN BAKED SEA BASS
- COURGETTE TERRINE
- WARM POTATO SALAD
- AMERICAN-STYLE CHEESECAKE WITH KIWI FRUIT

A cool green theme for the recipe ingredients and lots of fresh herbs makes this menu light, delicious and perfect for a supper party on a balmy summer evening. The dishes can be served all at once, as a cold buffet, allowing guests to pick and choose as they like. On the other hand, if you prefer a more traditional menu plan, the asparagus makes a sumptuous starter and the other dishes a delicious main course, followed by pudding.

Sea bass done in a Mediterranean style is no more difficult to cook than salmon; simply wrap it in foil and bake. The flavour is better if you can cook the fish with the head on because fewer juices are lost. So, consider the size of your oven and pick your fish carefully.

To accompany it, I've created a classic salad of thin sticks of asparagus mixed with chopped hard-boiled eggs, chives and lemon juice. A courgette terrine drizzled with a tarragon dressing also teams up well with fish. Add a freshly made warm potato salad tossed in a herb vinaigrette, and you have the perfect plateful.

An American-style cheesecake is an easy-to-assemble grand finale. Made with cottage cheese and set with gelatine, it has a very light texture. The cheesecake mixture goes into the mould first and then the biscuit crumbs go on top. Once chilled and set, the cheesecake is turned out so the biscuit top becomes the base. Just finish it with sliced kiwi fruit to keep the green theme going!

timeplan

The day before

Make cheesecake and bake courgette terrine and refrigerate both. Prepare tarragon dressing and garlic mayonnaise.

Early in the morning

Bake sea bass and leave to cool in a foil parcel. Make asparagus salad with dressing. Unmould cheesecake and keep chilled.

About 1 hour before

Slice terrine on platter; arrange fish on platter and get out garlic mayonnaise. Make potato salad.

Last minute

Decorate cheesecake and spoon dressing over terrine. Add herb bouquet to fish platter.

Asparagus with chopped eggs

Make the most of home-produced asparagus while it's in season.

1.5 kg (3 lb) fresh asparagus

For the dressing
1 tablespoon white wine
   vinegar
1 tablespoon lemon juice
Salt and freshly milled pepper
1 teaspoon coarse-grain
   mustard
75 ml (3 fl oz) olive oil
3 tablespoons chopped chives
4 hard-boiled eggs

Rinse the asparagus and trim to the same length. Tie in bundles with 2.5 cm (1 in) wide gauze bandage for easy handling.

Drop the asparagus bundles into a pan of boiling salted water – large enough for the stalks to lie flat. Simmer gently for 8–10 minutes – test by piercing a stalk with a knife. When it's ready, lift the asparagus from the pan. Drain on a clean tea cloth. Loosen the bundles and arrange on a serving platter.

In a mixing bowl stir together the wine vinegar, lemon juice, salt and milled pepper and the mustard, then stir in the oil. Add the chives and mix. Pour the dressing over the hot asparagus and cool to room temperature. Shell the eggs, then cut them in half. Chop the egg whites and yolks separately, then sprinkle over the asparagus and serve.

Mediterranean baked sea bass

Baking in foil is by far the easiest way of cooking a whole fish.

2 sea bass about 700–900 g
(1½–2 lb) each, scaled and
gutted
Salt and freshly milled pepper
Olive oil and slices of lemon
Juice ½ lemon
50 ml (2 fl oz) olive oil
6–8 black olives
Flatleaf parsley bouquet

For the garlic mayonnaise

1 clove garlic
175 ml (6 fl oz) mayonnaise
2 tablespoons soured cream

Your fishmonger will prepare the fish for you. Rinse the fish inside and out, and pat dry. Season inside the fish with salt and pepper. Rub the outside with olive oil.

Heat the oven to 200°C/400°F/Gas Mark 6. Set each fish on a large square of oiled foil and add 2–3 slices of lemon. Draw the foil up and over the fish and seal by folding along the top to make a baggy parcel. Slide both fish on to a baking tray. Bake in the oven for 40 minutes. Remove the fish from the oven but do not open the foil as it needs to cool for 4–6 hours. Mix the lemon juice with the olive oil.

Open each foil parcel carefully. Peel away the skin. Transfer the fish to a serving platter. Season with pepper, drizzle with the lemon oil, scatter a few olives and add parsley bouquet for decoration.

To serve: snipping through the bone at the head and tail end allows you to lift out the bone and you can reach the fillets on the underside. Using a palette knife, lift off the fish fillets and offer with garlic mayonnaise.

Garlic mayonnaise: for a mild flavour, bruise the garlic clove and rub it around the inside of the bowl. Remove and discard it. Spoon in your favourite prepared mayonnaise, and add the soured cream. Stir and season to taste.

Katie's tip
Presenting a whole fish at the table is something of a challenge. I find that putting it on leaves is very fresh looking – take two of the longest Cos lettuce leaves, arrange end to end and place the fish on top, letting the leaf edges curl around it. Bright green, blanched samphire grass makes a pretty garnish. Or use a bouquet of fresh herbs tied with fine string.

Courgette terrine

A vegetable terrine teams up perfectly with cold fish or meat.

2–3 tablespoons chopped
   flatleaf parsley
1 medium onion
500 g (1 lb 2 oz) courgettes
2 tablespoons olive oil
2 tablespoons chopped
   tarragon
25 g (1 oz) grated Parmesan
50 g (2 oz) fresh white
   breadcrumbs
3 eggs
150 ml (5 fl oz) double
   cream
Salt and freshly milled pepper

For the tarragon dressing

6 tablespoons olive oil
2 tablespoons white wine
   vinegar
1 teaspoon Dijon mustard
1 tablespoon unchopped
   tarragon leaves
Salt and freshly milled pepper

Select an oblong terrine or baking pan with a 1 litre (1¾ pint) capacity. Lightly oil the mould and line the base with oiled greaseproof paper. Sprinkle the inside of the mould with the chopped parsley. Shake out any that doesn't adhere.

Peel and finely chop the onion. Top and tail the courgettes but do not peel them, then cut in chunks. Heat the oil in a large frying-pan, add the onion and allow to soften. Add the courgettes, chopped tarragon and any leftover parsley. Cover and cook gently to soften the courgettes – about 10–12 minutes. Draw off the heat and allow to cool.

Heat the oven to 180°C/350°F/Gas Mark 4. Turn the courgette mixture, grated Parmesan, breadcrumbs, eggs, cream and seasoning into a food processor bowl. Cover and whiz to a green speckled purée. Pour the courgette mixture into the prepared tin and spread level. Set in a large roasting tin with boiling water to come about 2.5 cm (1 in) up the sides of the terrine. Set in the oven and bake for 45–50 minutes or until the terrine has set. Allow to cool, then chill until serving. Loosen the sides and un-mould. Remove the lining paper, slice the terrine on to a serving platter and spoon over the tarragon dressing.

For the tarragon dressing: combine all the ingredients.

Warm potato salad

This salad is unusual and tastes wonderful when freshly made.

*1 kg (2¼ lb) English new
  potatoes
3 tablespoons white wine
  vinegar
2 tablespoons coarse-grain
  mustard
1 tablespoon clear honey
100 ml (3½ fl oz) olive oil
Salt and freshly milled pepper
1 bunch spring onions
3 tablespoons chopped flatleaf
  parsley*

Rinse the new potatoes. Add to a pan of boiling salted water and cook until tender – about 15 minutes. Drain and turn the potatoes on to a clean tea cloth to dry. Slice the potatoes thickly and turn into a serving bowl.

   Combine the vinegar, mustard, honey, olive oil and seasoning. Mix well, pour over the hot potatoes and turn them gently to coat all over. Trim the spring onions, then chop all the white and some of the green stems. Add them to the potato salad along with the chopped parsley. Mix again. Serve while still warm or at room temperature.

American-style cheesecake with kiwi fruit

The mousse-like texture and tangy lemon flavour make a perfect finale.

8 digestive biscuits
50g (2 oz) butter
25g (1 oz) soft brown sugar

For the cheesecake

350 g (12 oz) natural cottage
*   cheese*
Grated rind and juice
*   2 lemons*
15g (½ oz) powdered gelatine
3 eggs
100 g (4 oz) caster sugar
150ml (5 fl oz) double cream
2–3 kiwi fruit or other green
*   fruits*

First prepare the biscuit base. Crush the biscuits to fine crumbs, and melt the butter in a pan. Off the heat, stir in the biscuit crumbs and brown sugar; reserve this for using later. Line the base of a 20 cm (8 in) deep cake tin with greaseproof paper.

Press the cottage cheese through a sieve into a large mixing bowl. Add the lemon rind. Measure 3 tablespoons of cold water into a teacup, sprinkle in the gelatine and allow mixture to soak for 5 minutes. Separate the eggs. Add the caster sugar to the egg yolks and stir until blended and creamy. Make the squeezed juice of the lemons up to 150 ml (5 fl oz) with cold water. Pour into a saucepan and bring almost to a simmer. Stir the hot liquid into the egg yolks and sugar, mix well and return the mixture to the saucepan. Add the soaked gelatine. Stir over a moderate heat, long enough for the gelatine to dissolve – do not allow the mixture to boil. Dip the base of the hot pan in cold water to reduce the heat and let the mixture cool for about 15 minutes.

Stir the egg, sugar and gelatine mixture into the cottage cheese and lemon, and blend. Set the bowl aside until the mixture begins to thicken – up to 45 minutes. Whisk the egg whites until stiff and beat the cream to a soft custard consistency. Fold both gently into the mixture. Pour into the prepared tin and spread level. Set aside 1 tablespoon of the reserved biscuit crumb mixture, then sprinkle the remainder evenly over the top of the cheesecake – when turned out this becomes the base. Chill for several hours or overnight.

To serve, loosen the sides of the cake tin with a knife and invert the cheesecake on to a serving plate. Carefully peel off the lining paper and decorate the top with pared and thinly sliced kiwi fruit and a light sprinkle of the biscuit crumb mixture.

Wine recommendations

Sauvignon Blanc makes a great wine for drinking with asparagus, the grassy green flavours of the grape doing justice to this rather grand vegetable. New Zealand is about the best, but the Loire, South Africa and Hungary produce some fine ones too. An unusual alternative would be Grüner Veltliner, a spicy dry white with bags of character from Austria. A gently buttery white with smooth contours and a nice savoury edge will work best with the sea bass. Light oaky Chardonnay from almost anywhere would be fine, or ring the changes by looking to Alsace Pinot Gris, Australian Sémillon or a white Côtes du Rhône. An Austrian Beerenauslese, top-value sweet wine that can be bought in half-bottles, would be a good match for the cheesecake.

Special Sunday lunch

A spread from the Med

Leave-it-to-cook lunch

Cold weather comfort food

Lunch Parties

SPECIAL
SUNDAY LUNCH

menu for 8

- HONEY-GLAZED ROAST LAMB WITH HONEY MINT SAUCE
- DAUPHINOISE POTATOES
- BRAISED LEEKS WITH HAZELNUTS
- STUFFED MUSHROOMS WITH PARMESAN
- RHUBARB AND ORANGE COMPOTE
- HOME-MADE VANILLA CUSTARD

When you invite friends over for Sunday lunch it's a time to relax over a glass of wine, not to be stuck in the kitchen among the pots and pans. With this in mind, I've planned my recipes for ease of cooking and with an emphasis on the more traditional dishes.

Roast lamb is an excellent choice, especially when partnered with rosemary and honey and a sauce using fresh mint. The honey glaze turns the joint a lovely golden colour, and the honey-sweetened mint sauce is a flavoursome change from the sharp vinegary taste of traditional recipes.

A hot gratin of thinly sliced potatoes in cream and milk with a hint of garlic, baked and served in the same dish, goes well with any roast and is a practical choice for a party occasion as it needs no supervision. Add my

The day before

Make rhubarb and orange compote and chill. Prepare hazelnut topping for leeks. Prepare stuffed mushrooms and chill.

In the morning

Make vanilla custard and honey mint sauce.

1-2 hours before

Prepare lamb and potatoes and put on to cook.

30 minutes before

Put mushrooms on to bake. Cook the leek dish.

Just before serving the pudding

Warm vanilla custard for serving.

timeplan

braised leeks with a crunchy topping of toasted hazelnuts and you have a mouth-watering combination.

Lots of families, mine included, have a vegetarian on board, so for this menu I have included some generous-sized mushrooms, stuffed with spring onion, cheese and herbs, which can be served along with the other vegetable dishes.

I've always loved rhubarb – whether early tender pink stalks or the later garden variety – so it's nice to see it come back into food fashion. Do please follow my recipe method to ensure the rhubarb remains in pretty pieces; add grated orange rind and the flavour is magic. Serve the resulting compote with a home-made vanilla custard sauce – this is just the occasion for something deliciously old-fashioned.

Honey-glazed roast lamb with honey mint sauce

When it's available, home-produced lamb is the most tender and
flavoursome; with this glaze and sweet mint sauce, it's a special treat.

2 tablespoons plain flour
1 teaspoon salt
Freshly milled black pepper
¼ teaspoon ground cinnamon
Bruised leaves of 2–3 sprigs
  fresh rosemary
1 whole leg of lamb, about
  2 kg (4½ lb)
1 large onion, peeled and
  thickly sliced
2 medium carrots, pared and
  thickly sliced
2 tablespoons clear honey
300 ml (10 fl oz) dry cider
1 tablespoon cornflour

For the honey mint sauce
100 ml (3½ fl oz) white
  wine vinegar
2 tablespoons clear honey
4–6 tablespoons fresh mint,
  finely chopped

Heat the oven to 180°C/350°F/Gas Mark 4. Combine the flour, salt, pepper, cinnamon and rosemary and rub well into the lamb on all sides. Lay the onion and carrot in the bottom of the roasting tin and the lamb on top. Roast, allowing 25–30 minutes per 500 g (1 lb 2 oz) weight – less for a pinker meat. Turn the joint halfway through to cook evenly.

Meanwhile, make the sauce: warm the vinegar and honey until the honey has dissolved, then stir in the mint and leave to cool.

About 30 minutes before the end of cooking time, carefully lift out the meat and strain off the fat from the roasting tin (leave the vegetables). Replace the meat, best side up. Spread with the honey and add the cider to the pan. Return to the oven, increasing the heat to 190°C/375°F/Gas Mark 5, and finish roasting, basting once or twice.

Lift the joint and vegetables on to a hot serving platter. Blend the cornflour with 1 tablespoon of cold water, add to the roasting tin and boil, stirring for a few minutes to make gravy. Strain into a hot sauceboat. Serve the lamb with the hot cider gravy and honey mint sauce.

Dauphinoise potatoes

Slide the potatoes into the oven under the roast lamb. Cover with foil only if they start to brown too quickly.

900 g (2 lb) potatoes
1 clove garlic, peeled and lightly crushed
75 g (3 oz) butter
300 ml (10 fl oz) whole milk
300 ml (10 fl oz) double cream
Salt and freshly milled black pepper
Pinch grated nutmeg

Peel the potatoes and slice thinly – use a mandolin slicer for speed. Don't rinse them or you'll wash off the starch that makes them creamy.

Heat the oven to 180°C/350°F/Gas Mark 4. Select a large baking dish – which the potatoes will also be served in. Rub the garlic round inside the baking dish. Generously grease the dish with about 25 g (1 oz) of the butter. Put the milk, cream, remaining butter, seasoning and nutmeg into a large pan. Bring to a simmer, add the potato slices and heat gently, bringing the contents back to a simmer.

Turn the contents of the pan into the baking dish and spread the potato slices evenly. Place in the oven and bake for 1–1½ hours or until the potatoes are tender and browned on the surface.

Braised leeks with hazelnuts

The leeks retain a beautiful green colour and taste deliciously nutty.

75 g (3 oz) skinned hazelnuts
75 g (3 oz) butter
100 g (4 oz) fresh white breadcrumbs
Salt and freshly milled black pepper
8 leeks

The hazelnut mixture can be made ahead. Toast the hazelnuts until golden – under the grill or in a hot oven. Chop coarsely in a food processor. Melt 50 g (2 oz) of the butter in a frying-pan, add the breadcrumbs and fry, stirring until golden. Draw off the heat, season and stir in the hazelnuts. Allow to cool and reserve until needed.

Trim the leeks, split lengthways, and rinse. Cut into 5 cm (2 in) pieces. Arrange in a 25 cm (10 in) frying-pan in one layer. Dot the rest of the butter on top and add 3 tablespoons of cold water. Cover and simmer over a moderate heat for 15 minutes or until tender.

Remove the pan lid and raise the heat to boil away excess liquid, leaving the leeks in the buttery juices. Season and sprinkle with the hazelnut mixture. Transfer to a warm serving dish.

cf. Mossiman's recipe
for stuffing - braised
onion, celery,

Stuffed mushrooms with Parmesan

These are a good vegetarian alternative to the lamb, but also make a tasty lunch or supper snack with salad.

8 large open mushrooms
6 thick-cut slices from a large white loaf, crusts removed
1 bunch spring onions
Grated rind 1 lemon
2 tablespoons chopped parsley
75 g (3 oz) grated Parmesan
Salt and freshly milled black pepper
Grated nutmeg
50 g (2 oz) butter, melted
1 egg
Paprika for dusting
2–3 tablespoons olive oil

Remove the stalks from the mushrooms (there is no need to peel them). Whiz bread slices to crumbs in a food processor and turn into a mixing bowl – you should have 200 g (7 oz) breadcrumbs.

Trim the spring onions, then chop all the white and some of the green stems. Add the onions, lemon rind, parsley, Parmesan and a seasoning of salt, milled pepper and nutmeg to the breadcrumbs. Stir in the melted butter with a fork.

Mix the egg with 2 tablespoons of cold water to break it up. Add to the stuffing mixture, stirring with a fork to moisten evenly. Take heaped tablespoons of the stuffing mixture and press into each open mushroom. Arrange the mushrooms in a single layer on an oiled baking tray or a baking dish. Dust generously with paprika. Chill until time to cook.

Heat the oven to 180°C/350°F/Gas Mark 4. Drizzle the stuffed mushrooms with olive oil, place in the oven and bake for 20–25 minutes. Serve hot.

Katie's tip

White or wholemeal breadcrumbs are useful to have on hand. They will keep for months sealed in a polythene bag in the freezer so it's worthwhile making up a quantity at a time. I buy a large, thick-sliced loaf, let it stand for a day (to become a little dry), then trim the crusts and whiz the whole loaf to crumbs in a food processor. They can be used from frozen – just shake out the amount required from the freezer pack.

Rhubarb and orange compote

This is wonderful made with the pink stalks of early rhubarb — the colour is glorious. I freeze cut-up stalks of raw, fresh rhubarb and make this out of season, adding frozen rhubarb directly to the hot syrup.

900 g (2 lb) fresh rhubarb
175 g (6 oz) caster sugar
Zest and juice 1 orange

Wash and trim the rhubarb, then cut the stalks into 2.5 cm (1 in) lengths. Measure 300 ml (10 fl oz) cold water into a large pan, add the sugar and stir over a low heat until dissolved. Bring to the boil and add the rhubarb. Bring back to a simmer and cook gently for 1–2 minutes. Immediately draw the pan off the heat, cover tightly with a lid and leave undisturbed for 15 minutes — the rhubarb will continue to soften while remaining in whole pieces. Test its tenderness with a knife tip.

Grate orange zest directly into the hot rhubarb, then add the juice. Transfer to a serving bowl. Leave until cold then chill — the flavour is even better after 24 hours. Serve with home-made vanilla custard or vanilla ice-cream.

Home-made vanilla custard

Use up the egg whites left over from this recipe for home-made meringues: make with unrefined icing sugar for a butterscotch flavour.

600 ml (1 pint) whole milk
1 vanilla pod
50 g (2 oz) caster sugar
1 tablespoon cornflour
4 egg yolks

Place the milk and vanilla pod in a pan and bring almost to the boil. Draw off the heat and infuse for 10 minutes, then remove the vanilla pod. In a small bowl, combine the sugar and cornflour and mix well. Add the egg yolks and mix until creamy. Gradually stir in the milk. Rinse out the milk pan (custard is less likely to catch in a clean, wet pan) and return the custard to the saucepan.

Set the custard over a moderate heat and bring to the boil, stirring — the cornflour stops the custard separating. Strain into a bowl and leave to cool — stir occasionally to prevent a skin forming. To warm for serving, pour the custard into a jug and stand in a pan of hot (not boiling) water.

Wine recommendations

Red wines made entirely or predominantly from Cabernet Sauvignon are the most fitting partners for roast lamb. Traditionally, a mature claret would be the accompaniment of choice, but they are expensive, and there are in any case some outstanding examples of Cabernet being produced all over the world now. Go for California, Chile or Australia as best sources. Alternatively, opt for a Rioja Reserva with a few years' bottle-age – another fine, classic match. Younger Cabernets will benefit from an hour or so in the decanter before serving. Rhubarb isn't the best friend of wine on account of its high acidity, but I have found a reasonably priced dry pink fizz from, say, Australia or New Zealand to go quite well with it.

A SPREAD
FROM THE MED

Get friends together for a Mediterranean-style lunch at the weekend, when you can linger over the table discussing holidays enjoyed or planned and delicious meals tasted abroad.

As guests arrive, set the scene with meze-style starters to pick at. A bowl of home-made chick pea and olive pâté and warm pitta bread is nicer than any hummus you can buy. It takes only a moment to purée the ingredients in a food processor. I use tinned chick peas and tahini, available in any supermarket. Marinated vegetables should be tender-crisp and look especially pretty with whole mini-vegetables and flavoursome olives mixed in. A butterflied leg of lamb (boned and opened out flat) is wonderful for a crowd and so easy to serve – just keep slicing. Marinate it in lemon and garlic beforehand and

The day before

Make chick pea and black olive pâté and cover with cling film. Prepare and marinate vegetables. Marinate butterflied lamb. Make polenta.

In the morning

Prepare aubergines and make your own basil pesto. Stuff peaches and set in baking dish. Arrange polenta on baking tray.

30 minutes before

Put lamb on to barbecue or grill. Put aubergines to roast.

Last minute

Grill polenta. Warm pitta bread. Start baking peaches 20-30 minutes before serving.

start cooking early: on the barbecue is best – so the wonderful aromas greet your guests as they arrive – though the recipe can be adapted for indoor cooking. I like to serve it with polenta, a good way of getting something starchy but interesting on the menu. You can make the polenta ahead and just grill to serve. Get out your best platter, line up the hot polenta on the dish alongside the sliced grilled lamb and offer roasted aubergines with pesto as a vegetable.

I've chosen hot peaches for dessert. Make sure the fruit you buy is ripe and ready to eat, otherwise it will be difficult to halve them and extract the stones – essential because the hollows are stuffed with a delicious macaroon mix. Don't bake them in advance: it's better to take the hot peaches straight to the table.

Chick pea and black olive pâté

This pâté should have a good balance of garlic and lemon – it's important to taste the prepared mixture and adjust the flavour to your liking.

400 g tin chick peas
3 cloves garlic
Salt and freshly milled pepper
2 tablespoons tahini (sesame seed paste)
2 tablespoons olive oil, plus extra for drizzling
Juice 1–2 lemons
10–12 pitted black olives
Paprika
Warmed pitta bread to serve

Drain and rinse the chick peas, then put into a food processor bowl. Peel and crush the garlic cloves, add to the chick peas with a seasoning of salt and milled pepper, the tahini, olive oil and lemon juice. Cover and blend to a purée. Check the flavour and add more salt, pepper or lemon juice, if necessary.

Cut the olives into slivers and mix into the chick pea and tahini purée. Turn the mixture into a serving bowl, lightly indent the top with a fork and drizzle over a little extra olive oil. Sprinkle with paprika and serve with the warmed pitta bread.

Crunchy marinated vegetables

These are intended as a nibble, but are also good as a salad.

1 small head cauliflower
4 tender young courgettes
200 g (7 oz) French beans
200 g (7 oz) baby carrots
100 g (4 oz) whole black olives
2 tablespoons chopped fresh oregano

For the marinade

175 ml (6 fl oz) olive oil
Juice 2 lemons
2 crushed cloves garlic
1 teaspoon dried herbes de Provence
1 teaspoon salt
6 whole black peppercorns, crushed
3 bay leaves

Prepare the vegetables according to their kind: separate the cauliflower head into small florets; trim but do not peel the courgettes – simply pare strips from the skin for effect and cut in chunks; if you like, leave the pretty tails on the beans and carrots. Steam the vegetables in batches for 6–8 minutes or until tender-crisp. Arrange in a medium-sized bowl.

In a small pan, bring all the marinade ingredients to the boil. Pour over the vegetables and cool the mixture to room temperature. Add the olives and oregano. Marinate for 24 hours. Serve with extra-crusty bread to dip into the marinade.

Butterflied leg of lamb

A whole leg is boned and opened out flat, marinated then grilled,
barbecued or roasted, so the meat is dark and crusty on the outside
and a delicate pink in the middle.

*1 leg of lamb, about 2 kg
(4½ lb)*

For the marinade
*Grated rind and juice
   2 lemons
4 tablespoons olive oil
2–3 peeled cloves garlic or
   sprigs of thyme*

Ask the butcher to bone the lamb for you, or do it yourself: set
the lamb on a steady chopping board with the shank end towards
you. Using a sharp knife, make a deep cut the length of the joint
and feel for the bone. Follow the bone, cutting around and under
until you can lift it out, then open the meat out flat. Score with a
knife, criss-cross fashion, on both sides.

For the marinade, mix together the lemon rind and juice and
olive oil in a shallow bowl. Add the garlic or thyme. Slide in the
boned meat and baste with the marinade. Cover and refrigerate for
24 hours, turning occasionally so the meat absorbs the flavour on
all sides.

Heat the grill to hot, line the grill pan with foil and set it
7.5 cm (3 in) below the heat source. Drain the lamb from the
marinade and open out on to the grill rack. Set under the heat
and grill the meat for 20 minutes each side, turning once.
Alternatively, heat the oven to 220°C/425°F/Gas Mark 7, open
the meat on to a rack in a roasting tin and roast for about 50
minutes. Let the meat rest for 10–15 minutes, then carve in slices
across the joint. Allow the slices to fall as they come from the
joint, then transfer together to a serving platter. Drizzle over any
meat juices and serve.

Katie's tip

An alternative to marinating meat (or poultry) for the barbecue or grill is to put the marinade ingredients in a suitably
sized freezer bag, add the meat, close securely and turn the bag over several times to coat. Slide the bag and its contents
on to a shelf in the refrigerator – it will take up less space than a bowl. Allow at least 4 hours for the flavours to develop,
or leave overnight (especially with joints), turning the bag several times, if possible.

Grilled polenta

I like polenta with flavours added, especially Parmesan. If you prefer, you can buy polenta ready flavoured with sun-dried tomatoes or herbs – simply follow the instructions on the packet.

250 g (9 oz) instant polenta
1 teaspoon salt
25 g (1 oz) butter
50 g (2 oz) grated Parmesan
8 sun-dried tomatoes in oil,
  drained and chopped
Freshly milled pepper
Grated nutmeg
Olive oil for grilling

Measure the polenta on to a square of greaseproof paper or foil. Bring 1 litre (1¾ pints) of cold water and the salt to the boil in a large pan. Then, stirring all the time, add the polenta in a slow, steady stream and bring back to the boil. Lower the heat to a simmer and cook for 1–2 minutes, stirring until the mixture is quite thick – be sure to take care at this stage, because boiling polenta tends to spit.

Remove the polenta from the heat, then stir in the butter and Parmesan, the sun-dried tomatoes and plenty of milled black pepper and nutmeg to season. Pour the polenta on to an oiled, flat baking tray or large plate and spread out to form a 2 cm (¾ in) thick cake, and slightly roughen the surface with a fork. Leave the polenta until it is completely cold, then cut into rough wedges.

Just before you want to serve the polenta to your guests, crowd the slices on to a baking tray. Drizzle with the extra olive oil and grill for 8 minutes, or until heated through and golden.

Roasted aubergine with pesto

Make your own pesto for this recipe (see below) – alternatively use any jar of ready-made basil pesto sauce.

4–5 slim, elongated
  aubergines
Sea salt
6–8 tablespoons olive oil
Basil pesto sauce for serving

Cut the aubergines into 2.5 cm (1 in) thick slices. Sprinkle with salt and leave in a colander for 30 minutes, then pat the slices dry. Rub 1–2 baking trays with olive oil. Put the slices in a bowl, drizzle over the remaining oil, turn them with your fingers to oil both sides and place on the trays.

Preheat the oven to 200°C/400°F/Gas Mark 6. Roast the slices for 30–35 minutes, turning once, until tender (test with a knife) and golden. Transfer to a platter, spoon pesto on to each slice and serve.

Classic basil pesto

40 g (1½ oz) basil leaves
  (2 small basil plants)
2 garlic cloves, peeled and
  sliced
25 g (1 oz) pinenuts
50 g (2 oz) Parmesan, grated
100 ml (3½ fl oz) olive oil
Salt and pepper

Put the basil leaves in a food processor with the garlic cloves. Add the pinenuts, Parmesan and salt and pepper. Cover and whiz to make a purée. With the processor running, pour in the olive oil to make a thick dressing. Don't over-process – the pesto shouldn't be completely smooth.

Wine recommendations

The citric tang of that dressing on the marinated vegetables doesn't have to present problems for wine, as long as you fight fire with fire, as it were. Go for a sappy, sharp-edged dry white such as Chenin Blanc from South Africa or the Loire, or Riesling from Alsace or New Zealand. Match the mood of the food by serving a richly fruity Italian red with good structure to accompany the main course. Chianti Classico or Chianti Rufina of Riserva quality will work well, or else head for Rosso di Montalcino or Rosso di Conero, which also have plenty of fruit-filled, peppery class. Stay with the Italian theme by serving well-chilled Asti with the baked peaches, a light and refreshing way to finish a lunch spread.

Italian baked peaches

Warm fruits have a special flavour, and these peach halves with a macaroon stuffing are very special indeed. Prepare ahead, then bake and serve hot from the baking dish.

100 g (4 oz) almond macaroons
25 g (1 oz) butter, at room temperature
50 g (2 oz) caster sugar
1 egg yolk
8 ripe peaches
4–6 tablespoons port or red wine

Crush the macaroons to coarse crumbs (in a polythene bag with a rolling pin is easiest). Cream the butter and sugar; stir in the egg yolk and macaroons.

Cut the peaches, following the natural line around the fruit from the stalk end, then twist the halves in opposite directions to separate. Remove the stones and scoop out a little of the pulp to make more space for the filling. Add the pulp to the stuffing mixture and combine with a fork. Press walnut-sized amounts of the mixture into each peach half.

Preheat the oven to 180°C/350°F/Gas Mark 4. Arrange the stuffed peaches in a single layer in a buttered gratin dish. Bake uncovered for about 25 minutes. While the peaches are still hot, spoon over the port or red wine to make delicious juices, then serve.

LEAVE-IT-TO-COOK LUNCH

Simple country produce cooked in a traditional manner and served with the minimum of fuss is the theme for this hearty lunch menu. Slow simmering really concentrates flavours, and recipes need little attention; get these dishes on the go and leave them to it. Butternut squash has long been a favourite of mine and works wonderfully with apple for a surprisingly good soup, subtly flavoured and with a glorious orange colour.

Follow the soup with a braise of lean pork loin steaks which cooks on its own and needs little attention. Here the pork is sweet and spicy, thanks to the addition of caramelized onion, prunes, spices and vinegar stirred in to sharpen up the taste. Partner the casserole with fresh plain egg noodles, flavoured with walnuts, to soak

up the rich gravy. And then be right up to date and serve cabbage with it. This leafy green traditionalist is making something of a comeback. I think our Savoy cabbage is one of the best, with a good colour and delicate flavour. Cabbage should be cooked briefly and takes perfectly to stir-frying – you can't overcook it using this simple method.

A home-made fruit pie or tart is the perfect dessert for this menu. Recently I've been trying out an interesting idea: a free-fold tart where the pastry is rolled out to a circle, topped with fruit and folded back over the filling. Once you get the hang of this easy fruit tart there will be no stopping you – try it with apples and blackberries or plums.

timeplan

The day before
Make butternut squash and apple soup, cool and refrigerate. Fry soup croutons, cool and store in airtight container.

In the morning
Assemble plum tart ready for baking. Prepare spiced pork loin steaks with prunes – this will reheat perfectly. Toast and chop walnuts for pasta.

45 minutes before
Put plum tart to bake. Reheat spiced pork lower down in oven.

Last minute
Stir-fry cabbage. Cook fresh noodles. Reheat butternut squash and apple soup.

Butternut squash and apple soup

Sprinkle soup with crunchy croutons for a satisfying lunch.

500 g (1 lb 2 oz) butternut
squash (or 1 large squash),
peeled and seeded
250 g (9 oz) carrots
1 medium onion
1 clove garlic
3 sharp-flavoured dessert
apples
50 g (2 oz) butter
1 litre (1¾ pints) vegetable
stock
Salt and freshly milled pepper
2–3 slices white bread for
croutons
25 g (1 oz) butter and
2 tablespoons olive oil for
frying
Coarsely cracked pepper

Cube the butternut squash. Peel and slice the carrots. Peel and chop the onion and peel and crush the garlic. Peel, core and cut up the apples.

In a large pan melt the butter and sauté the onion to soften. Stir in the garlic, squash and carrots and cook for 5 minutes. Add the apples and stock. Bring to a simmer and cook for 30 minutes or until the vegetables are tender. Whiz in a blender or food processor to a golden purée and check the seasoning with salt and freshly milled pepper.

Trim the crusts from the bread slices and cut the slices into dice for croutons. Quickly fry the croutons in the hot butter and oil, stirring constantly, until golden brown and crisp. Lift from the pan and drain on kitchen paper.

Reheat the butternut squash and apple soup and serve it in warmed bowls. Garnish with a scattering of crunchy croutons and a sprinkle of coarsely cracked pepper.

Katie's tip

All apples are suitable for cooking, although they react in different ways. 'Dessert' apples are the ones to choose if you want to preserve whole chunks of fruit for poaching, while the more acidic 'cooking' apples collapse quickly and efficiently to a purée – the ones to choose for apple sauce. For pies, crumbles and baked puddings, any type of apple can be used as long as you make allowances for differing degrees of sweetness. The more tart-flavoured varieties of 'dessert' apples are excellent cut up into salads and soups and added to casseroles where the flavour complements other savoury ingredients. Apples are versatile and very compatible – hazelnuts or almonds, spices, herbs such as thyme or sage, citrus fruit zest, raisins, dates and quinces are all excellent partners for flavour.

Spiced pork loin steaks with prunes

Pork loin steaks in a casserole make for easy individual servings. The caramelized onions, mildly spiced gravy and prunes all add to the rich flavour.

2 large onions
6 pork loin steaks
3 tablespoons seasoned flour
2 tablespoons olive oil
2 tablespoons granulated
  sugar
½ teaspoon ground allspice
½ teaspoon ground cinnamon
2 tablespoons red wine
  vinegar
2–3 bay leaves
100 g (4 oz) ready-to-eat,
  dried, pitted prunes
400 ml (14 fl oz) vegetable
  stock
Salt and freshly milled pepper

Heat the oven to 160°C/325°F/Gas Mark 3. Peel and thinly slice the onions. Dip the meat in the seasoned flour. Heat the olive oil in a roomy frying-pan, add the pork steaks and brown each one on both sides. Transfer to a large casserole.

Add the onions to the hot oil and stir to soften over a moderate heat. Add the sugar and stir until the onions caramelize. Stir in the spices, vinegar and 2 tablespoons of cold water. Simmer until the onions are syrupy – about 2–3 minutes. Pour the caramelized onions over the pork. Add the bay leaves, prunes and stock. Cover with the casserole lid, set in the heated oven and cook for 1½ hours. Season with salt and freshly milled pepper to taste before serving.

Stir-fried green cabbage

Stir-frying is simple and takes only a moment. Using this method also avoids overcooked or soggy cabbage.

1 teaspoon caraway seeds
3 tablespoons olive oil
700 g (1½ lb) Savoy
  cabbage, finely shredded
75 ml (3 fl oz) vegetable
  stock
Salt and freshly milled pepper

Heat a dry wok or 25 cm (10 in) frying-pan over a moderate heat. Add the caraway seeds and toast them for a moment, then tip them on to a plate.

Put the oil into the hot pan and add the shredded cabbage. Stir-fry for 2–3 minutes until the cabbage is bright green and glossy. Add the vegetable stock, stir and cook for 2–3 minutes; the volume of the cabbage will reduce as it cooks. The shreds should be tender-crisp. Add the caraway seeds, a seasoning of salt and milled pepper, stir up and then serve.

Buttered fresh noodles with walnuts

Use fresh tagliatelle or fettuccine in this recipe. Be sure to tease the pasta strands out before adding them to the cooking water and they will be less likely to clump together.

100 g (4 oz) walnut pieces
1 x 500 g pack fresh
  tagliatelle or fettuccine
Salt
25 g (1 oz) butter
Freshly milled pepper

For extra flavour, I always start by toasting the walnut pieces. Simply place them on a baking tray in a hot oven for 4–6 minutes or under the grill. Then with a sharp kitchen knife chop them into fine pieces.

Add the fresh pasta to a large pan with plenty of boiling salted water – about 3 litres (5½ pints). Bring back to the boil, stirring, then let the pasta cook for 3–5 minutes until tender. Drain well in a colander.

Turn the pasta into a heated serving dish, add the butter and a good seasoning of milled pepper and toss to glaze the pasta. Sprinkle it liberally with the chopped toasted walnuts. Toss again on serving.

Free-fold plum tart

I use my mother's old-fashioned enamel pie plate here. You may well find that you have one lurking in the kitchen cupboard. If not, you can shape this plum tart directly on a baking tray.

175 g (6 oz) plain flour
75 g (3 oz) butter
Milk and granulated sugar, for
*   decorating*
Icing sugar, for dusting

For the filling

50 g (2 oz) skinned
*   hazelnuts*
1 kg (2¼ lb) red or purple
*   plums*
2–3 tablespoons caster sugar
1 tablespoon cornflour
Grated nutmeg
15 g (½ oz) butter in flakes

Sift the flour into a mixing bowl. Add the butter in pieces and rub in gently using only the fingertips. Sprinkle over 2 tablespoons of cold water and stir to moisten the mix. With floured fingers, draw the ingredients together to form a dough. Turn the dough out on to a floured work surface and knead gently for a moment. Cover and chill the dough for 30 minutes.

Toast the skinned hazelnuts, then whiz in a blender to make fine crumbs. Cut the plums in half, along the natural line, and twist the halves in opposite directions to separate. Remove the stones and slice the plums into a mixing bowl. Combine the caster sugar, cornflour and a seasoning of nutmeg. Sprinkle over the fruits and toss to mix.

Roll the pastry to a circle large enough to line a 23 cm (9 in) buttered pie plate with 5 cm (2 in) to spare all round. Trim the pastry if uneven. Transfer the pastry to the pie plate, allowing the excess to overhang the edge. Spread the ground hazelnuts over the tart base – the nuts will absorb excess fruit juices and keep the base crust dry. Pile on the plums with flakes of butter and spread out evenly. Fold the pastry edges inwards around the rim, leaving the centre of the tart uncovered.

Heat the oven to 200°C/400°F/Gas Mark 6. Brush the pastry with milk and sprinkle with granulated sugar. Set the tart in the heated oven and bake for 40–45 minutes. Cool slightly, then dust the pastry rim with icing sugar and serve with cream.

Wine recommendations

The best choice for a wine to go with soup is to serve a small measure of one of the drier fortified wines, to prevent too liquid a combination. This autumnal soup would be best served by one of the darker examples, such as Sercial Madeira or bone-dry amontillado sherry. A medium-bodied red with masses of fresh, youthful fruit will do justice to the pork and prune casserole. Pinot Noir from New Zealand or California or Pinotage from South Africa will fit the bill, as would a ripely brambly Merlot from Chile. The plum tart needs a reasonably light dessert wine. Late-harvested Muscats from the United States, Australia or Alsace (where they are labelled Vendange Tardive) will provide the right sort of weight.

COLD WEATHER COMFORT FOOD

menu for 6

- MONKFISH GUMBO
- WALNUT SODA BREAD
- MIXED LEAVES WITH BACON AND WHITE STILTON
- CHICORY, CARROT AND APPLE SLAW
- GOLDEN SYRUP PUDDING

There's nothing more enjoyable at the weekend than having a relaxed round-the-kitchen-table lunch with friends – nothing too complicated, but every morsel of food full of flavour.

My monkfish gumbo is a hearty soup, with chunks of succulent fish and vegetables, and served with rice. Monkfish works best, but you could use firm-fleshed halibut or hoki if you prefer. Gumbo can be cooked within the hour. In fact, it should really be prepared and eaten straightaway.

It's surprisingly easy to make my walnut soda bread; mix and put a loaf in the oven and your guests will find the smell of home baking irresistible. Simply break the bread in quarters and slice – I like a little butter on

mine. Let friends dig into the two salads – both are delicious with the warm soda bread. Crunchy and fresh-tasting carrot and apple slaw is a simple salad that's one of my favourites for winter. Mixed leaves with bacon and white Stilton has bold, crunchy croutons, so there's texture and substance here.

My choice for dessert is an old-fashioned golden syrup pudding, made with a light sponge-cake mixture, steamed conveniently in the oven and served with a delicious syrup sauce – surprisingly lemony and not too sweet. An added bonus is that the pudding will keep hot without spoiling; if people are chatting, leave it covered and unmould only when you're ready to serve it. I guarantee it'll have your guests scraping their plates!

The day before

Combine ingredients for soda bread except for yoghurt mixture. Combine salad leaves and refrigerate in a sealed polythene bag. Make croutons, crisp bacon and crumble Stilton. Make both salad dressings. Combine chicory, carrot and spring onion for the slaw and refrigerate in a sealed polythene bag.

In the morning

Make the gumbo up to the stage before the fried fish and prawns are added. Leave to cool.

1 hour before

Mix syrup pudding and steam in oven. Prepare syrup sauce.

Last minute

Cook rice. Mix and bake soda bread. Grate apple for the slaw, then mix and toss both salads. Reheat gumbo, add fish and remaining ingredients, and cook.

Monkfish gumbo

Ideally, serve in old-fashioned shallow soup plates to show off the delicious and colourful contents.

1 medium onion
1 green pepper
3 sticks celery
2 cloves garlic
200 g (7 oz) okra
700 g (1½ lb) monkfish fillet
1 tablespoon plain flour
2 teaspoons paprika
2 tablespoons olive oil
3 tablespoons chopped parsley
1 litre (1¾ pints) vegetable
   stock
1 x 400 g tin chopped
   tomatoes
Freshly milled pepper
200 g (7 oz) prawns, cooked
   and peeled
Juice 1 lemon
Dash Tabasco
250 g (9 oz) cooked long-
   grain rice, to serve

Peel and finely chop the onion. Halve, deseed and chop the pepper. Snap the celery sticks and pull away the strings, then cut lengthways and across to chop small. Peel and crush the garlic. Trim the okra and slice diagonally. Cut the monkfish into chunky pieces. Combine the flour and paprika on a plate and roll the fish in the mixture to coat.

Heat the oil in a large pan, add the fish and fry until brown all over. Lift the fish from the pan and reserve on a plate. Add the onion, pepper, celery, garlic and parsley to the hot pan, stir and fry gently for about 5 minutes to soften. Add the okra, vegetable stock, tomatoes and seasoning. Bring to the boil, then lower the heat to a simmer and cook for 15 minutes.

Return the monkfish and juices to the pan. Add the prawns, lemon juice and a good dash of Tabasco to taste. Simmer for a further 3–5 minutes. To serve, warm the soup plates. Place a good tablespoonful of cooked rice in each plate, to one side, then ladle in the monkfish gumbo.

Katie's tip

If you don't want to go to the trouble of making your own stock, I highly recommend Marigold Swiss vegetable bouillon powder. It's widely available in supermarkets and health-food shops, and nowadays there's an organic version too. If you prefer, you can buy cartons of fresh chilled stock.

Walnut soda bread

Use diluted natural yoghurt in place of the traditional soured milk when making soda bread and you'll find the result is excellent.

225 g (8 oz) plain flour
225 g (8 oz) wholemeal flour
3 teaspoons baking powder
1 teaspoon salt
50 g (2 oz) butter, cut into pieces
50 g (2 oz) chopped walnuts
150 ml (5 fl oz) natural low-fat yoghurt
1 tablespoon finely chopped rosemary leaves, optional

Sift the flours, baking powder and salt into a large mixing bowl, then tip in the bran particles from the sieve. Add the butter and rub in with your fingertips. Add the walnuts.

Make the yoghurt up to 350 ml (12 fl oz) with cold water. Heat the oven to 200°C/400°F/Gas Mark 6. Pour all the liquid into the dry ingredients and, using a table knife, mix to a soft dough. Turn the dough on to a lightly floured work surface and, with floured fingers, knead gently. Place the dough, smooth side up, on a floured baking tray and pat into a round about 4 cm (1½ in) deep. With a floured kitchen knife, cut a deep cross in the bread to encourage even baking. Dip your fingers in water and moisten the top of the loaf. Sprinkle with rosemary, if using.

Bake in the oven for 25–30 minutes or until risen – the bread should sound hollow when tapped on the base. Transfer to a cooling rack.

Mixed leaves with bacon and white Stilton

A tasty combination of crisp bacon, crumbled cheese and crunchy croutons contrasts appetizingly with the salad leaves.

1 mini baguette
2–3 tablespoons olive oil
1 Iceberg lettuce
1 x 40 g pack rocket leaves
1 x 20 g pack flatleaf parsley
225 g (8 oz) streaky bacon
* rashers*
200 g (7 oz) white Stilton

For the dressing

1 tablespoon white wine
* vinegar*
3 tablespoons olive oil
Salt and freshly milled pepper
1 clove garlic

Heat the oven to 200°C/400°F/Gas Mark 6. Cut the baguette into thin slices; not more than 5 mm (¼ in) – you may not need the whole loaf. Toss the bread slices in olive oil and place on a baking tray. Toast in the oven for 8–10 minutes or until they are crunchy and brown.

Cut the lettuce in half and then into chunks. Pick over the rocket and coarsely chop the parsley. Combine the salad leaves, place in a polythene bag and tie the top, then refrigerate to crisp them up.

Trim the bacon rashers, then cut into small pieces. Blanch the bacon in boiling water for 1 minute, then drain and press dry in absorbent kitchen paper – this gets rid of the milky liquid that comes out of bacon when it's fried. Transfer the bacon to a dry frying-pan and sauté gently until crisp. Drain on kitchen paper. Crumble the Stilton into chunks.

Combine the vinegar, olive oil and seasoning. Cut the garlic clove in half and add to the mixture. Allow to stand for 1 hour, then remove the garlic – the flavour will be mild.

Turn the salad leaves into a bowl. Add the dressing and toss. Sprinkle the bacon, cheese and croutons on top, toss and serve.

Chicory, carrot and apple slaw

Chicory has a faintly bitter flavour, but if you cut out its core and mix it with apple you won't notice it at all.

4 chicory heads
3 medium carrots
2 bunches spring onions
2 green-skinned, tart, juicy dessert apples
1 teaspoon caster sugar
3 tablespoons olive oil
1 tablespoon white wine vinegar
Salt and freshly milled pepper
1 x 20 g pack flatleaf parsley

Trim the chicory heads, then cut in half lengthways and remove the core. Cut the chicory across the leaves into 1 cm (½ in) slices and separate out the layers. Put the shreds in a salad bowl. Peel and coarsely grate the carrots. Trim the spring onions, then chop all the white and some of the green stems. Pare, core and grate the apples. Add the carrot, onion and apple to the bowl. Sprinkle with sugar, which will draw the juices from the apple, and toss to mix.

Mix the olive oil, vinegar and seasoning and add to the salad. Coarsely chop the parsley leaves, add to the salad and toss again.

Golden syrup pudding

There's nothing more delicious on wintry days than an old-fashioned pudding. So go on, treat yourself ...

1 teaspoon golden syrup
175 g (6 oz) self-raising flour
Pinch salt
100 g (4 oz) butter
100 g (4 oz) golden caster
  sugar
Grated rind 1 lemon
2 eggs
2 tablespoons milk

For the syrup sauce
6 tablespoons golden syrup
Juice 1 lemon

To serve
Natural Greek-style yoghurt

Heat the oven to 190°C/375°F/Gas Mark 5. Butter a 900 ml (1½ pint) pudding basin and put the teaspoonful of golden syrup in the base. Sift the flour and salt on to a sheet of greaseproof paper. In a mixing bowl, cream the butter, sugar and lemon rind until soft and light. In another bowl, mix the eggs with a fork. Gradually beat the egg into the creamed mixture, adding a little of the flour with the last few additions of egg. Add the remaining flour and the milk and mix to a soft consistency. Spoon into the pudding bowl and spread level.

Lightly butter a square of foil large enough to cover the basin. Place the foil on top, tuck it securely around the edge and fasten with an elastic band around the rim. Place the pudding in a roasting tin. Cut a piece of foil to cover the tin and the basin. Pour boiling water from the kettle into the tin to a depth of 2.5 cm (1 in). Place the foil on top and tuck it under the edges of the tin to keep the steam in. Steam the pudding in the oven for 1 hour – you won't need to top up the water.

For the sauce, warm the syrup and lemon juice in a pan until thin and runny. Remove the foil from the tin, then from the pudding. Run a knife around the inside edge of the basin to loosen the pudding, then turn it on to a warmed serving plate. Spoon 2–3 tablespoons of the hot syrup over the pudding. Serve the remaining syrup separately, with slices of golden syrup pudding and spoonfuls of yoghurt.

Wine recommendations

The gumbo is one of those obliging dishes that will be as happy with a dry white wine as with a red. If white's your preference, choose a fairly sturdy creature with plenty of body, such as a white Rioja Crianza or even oaky white burgundy, to stand up to the meaty texture of the fish. The tomatoes in the recipe will also allow for a soft-textured red with supple tannins, though. Spain could provide the answer again, from somewhere like Valdepeñas, or try one of the blended reds of southern Portugal, from Ribatejo or Alentejo. Bring out your sweetest and stickiest stuff for golden syrup pudding: it will need nothing less. Austrian Beerenauslese or the equivalent noble-rotted wines from Australia or California will serve the purpose.

A moveable feast

The sophisticated picnic

Table under the trees

Outdoor Eating

A MOVEABLE FEAST

menu for 6

- PEPPERED TIGER PRAWNS WITH DILL MAYONNAISE

- BROWN BREAD AND LETTUCE SANDWICHES

- DUCK SALAD WITH SPICED PEARS AND SWEET SOY DRESSING

- MARINATED TOMATO SALAD

- NEW POTATO AND HERB SALAD

- RASPBERRY AND PECAN MUFFINS

Picnics are a wonderful way to entertain: eating in the open air makes everyone sociable, I find. As for the cook – well, all the hard work is behind you, so you can really relax and enjoy the party. For a smart occasion I like to go for buffet-style food which is easy to eat, dainty and colourful. This picnic menu is unfailingly popular among my friends: succulent tiger prawns with a dill mayonnaise dip to start with, followed by roast duck, which is always nice served cold, with a delicious dressing. Duck breast fillets are easy and quick to roast and always tender.

My clever brown bread and lettuce sandwiches combine two items – bread and salad – in one mouthful. Apart from anything else, they relieve you of carrying yet more bowls and plates.

I like to arrange picnic food on nice china and transport it ready to serve, protected with cling film, so

timeplan

The day before

Make dill mayonnaise for
peppered prawns.
Roast duck breast fillets
and cool. Prepare and
skin tomatoes for salad.
Make sandwiches, leave
untrimmed, wrap and
refrigerate. Prepare spiced
pears. Bake muffins.
Thaw tiger prawns in
refrigerator overnight.

Early on the day

Make new potato and
herb salad. Prepare tomato
salad. Assemble duck
salad – keep sweet soy
dressing separate. Stir-fry
tiger prawns. Trim, cut and
skewer sandwiches.

that I can whip the spread smartly from the basket. And
don't forget to tuck in a pretty tablecloth, napkins and
all the right accessories to back up your grand efforts.
Pack picnic foods in reverse order of use. Put the
muffins in a container at the bottom, the duck and salad
in the middle, then the prawns with dip and skewered
bread sandwiches on top. This way you won't have to
ferret around finding things. The soy dressing for the
duck salad and the dill mayonnaise dip for the prawns
are better carried separately in screw-topped jars – turn
the dip into a bowl and spoon the dressing over the
duck salad on site.

Last of all, pass the wonderful raspberry pecan
muffins for your guests to hold in their fingers and
nibble at – the bright red blobs of baked raspberry make
them delicious and moist.

Peppered tiger prawns with dill mayonnaise

These are raw prawn tails, shelled, turned in olive oil with cracked pepper then stir-fried until pink and cooked. The pepper makes them speckled but not fiercely hot. Eat them with your fingers and dip.

*3 x 200 g packs frozen
raw tiger prawn tails, with
shells on
3 tablespoons grapeseed or
other light oil
1 tablespoon cracked black
pepper*

For the dill mayonnaise dip

*150 ml (5 fl oz) mayonnaise
1 tablespoon coarse grain
mustard
1 teaspoon clear honey
2 tablespoons chopped fresh dill
Salt and freshly milled black
pepper*

Thaw the prawns overnight in the refrigerator. Carefully peel them, leaving on the tiny tail tips if possible. With a knife tip cut each prawn along the centre back, just piercing the skin – this encourages them to 'butterfly' and puff up prettily as they cook. Turn into a mixing bowl. Add the oil and coat the prawns. Sprinkle in the pepper and turn the prawns again – they will be speckled with pepper grains.

Heat a dry frying-pan over a moderate heat, add the prawns – about half at a time – and stir-fry until pink and cooked. Scoop the prawns from the pan and let them cool. Combine the mayonnaise, mustard, honey and dill, taste and season. To serve, spoon the dill mayonnaise into a bowl and offer with the peppered prawns for dipping.

Katie's tip

Uncooked prawns have a translucent, grey appearance – cooked prawns are bright pink. Raw prawns in their shells are delicious cooked on a barbecue, but for recipes you need to remove the shells. Twist off the heads, then peel back the legs and shell. I like to leave the tiny tails on so you can hold them for dipping. It is also important to remove any black line down the back. Raw, warm-water prawns are likely to have been imported frozen and thawed for sale. You should refrigerate, cook and eat thawed raw prawns within 24 hours. If you want to keep them in the freezer, buy frozen. Packs of raw prawn tails are good value as you're not paying for the heads.

Brown bread and lettuce sandwiches

Simple brown bread and butter sandwiches filled with lettuce and seasoned are delicious on a picnic with foods like home-cooked ham, rare roast beef, duck salad, or prawns. You could replace the lettuce with chopped chives, tarragon or dill and serve with gravadlax, cooked quails' eggs or egg mayonnaise. Lemon zest added to the butter makes them extra good with smoked salmon. Make the day before and, to pack, trim, cut into quarters, spear on satay sticks and wrap in greaseproof paper.

Duck salad with spiced pears and sweet soy dressing

Dark soy sauce is an excellent seasoning – I love it with roast duck
or grilled steaks. Kikkoman's sweet soy sauce is delicious in this dressing;
if using plain soy sauce add an extra tablespoon of muscovado sugar.

6 duck breast fillets
1 tablespoon honey
1 tablespoon dark soy sauce
3 heads chicory
1 x 85 g bag watercress
*100 ml (3½ fl oz) grapeseed
  or other light oil*
*3 tablespoons red wine
  vinegar*
*1 tablespoon light muscovado
  sugar*
*1 tablespoon dark sweet soy
  sauce*
1 clove garlic
*1 tablespoon chopped fresh
  coriander*

For the spiced pears

*4–6 medium-sized unripe
  Conference pears*
*175 g (6 oz) unrefined
  golden caster sugar*
1 stick cinnamon
4 cloves
6 thin slices fresh ginger
*2–3 pieces pared lemon rind
  and juice 1 lemon*

Heat the oven to 200°C/400°F/Gas Mark 6. Prick the skin on
each duck fillet with a fork. Mix the honey and soy sauce and
brush all over the duck skins. Set the duck fillets skin-side-up on a
rack in a baking dish or roasting tin. Add 2 tablespoons of cold
water to the container. Roast for 35–40 minutes – the skins should
be golden and the meat still a little pink. Allow to cool.

With a knife tip remove the core from the stalk end of each
chicory head, then shred across the leaves in slices. Separate out
the shreds. Pick over the watercress, discarding stalky bits. For the
dressing, combine the oil, vinegar, sugar and sweet soy sauce and
mix well. Peel the garlic clove and flatten with a knife blade. Add
to the dressing and allow it to flavour the mixture until serving
time. Then scoop out the garlic and add the chopped coriander.

Meanwhile, prepare the pears. First choose a pan into which
6 medium-sized pears will fit snugly so they will be covered with
the syrup. Measure 600 ml (1 pint) cold water into the pan, add
the sugar, spices and lemon rind and stir over a low heat to
dissolve the sugar. Peel the pears, leaving them whole with stalks
intact. As each pear is peeled, drop it into the pan. Replace the pan
over the heat and bring to a simmer, half cover with the pan lid
and cook pears gently until tender – about 30–40 minutes; test
with a knife tip. Add the lemon juice and allow the pears to cool
in the syrup before removing them for the duck salad.

To assemble the salad, thinly slice the duck fillets lengthways.
Cut the pears in quarters lengthways. To serve, scatter the chicory
and watercress on a serving platter. Add the duck and pears, then
spoon over the dressing.

Marinated tomato salad

This is the continental way to make a tomato salad. It's good for picnics but also excellent as a starter for a summer menu – pass round hot crusty bread to mop up the juices.

1 kg (2¼ lb) vine-ripened
    tomatoes
1 bunch spring onions
1 teaspoon caster sugar
Salt and freshly milled black
    pepper
1 tablespoon red wine vinegar
4 tablespoons olive oil

Cut out the stalk from each tomato. Scald the tomatoes in boiling water and pull away the skins. Slice crossways and place in a bowl. Trim the onions and chop all the white part and some of the green stems. Add to the bowl. Sprinkle with the sugar, season, and add the vinegar. Toss and marinate for at least 1 hour – the seasoning will draw juices from the tomatoes and the flavours will mingle. Before serving, spoon over the olive oil.

New potato and herb salad

Small new potatoes mixed while hot with a summery herby vinaigrette.

1 kg (2¼ lb) small new
  potatoes
1 bunch spring onions
1 teaspoon Dijon mustard
2 tablespoons white wine
  vinegar
75 ml (3 fl oz) grapeseed or
  other light oil
Salt and freshly milled black
  pepper
2 tablespoons finely chopped
  parsley
2 tablespoons snipped chives

Rinse the potatoes, add to boiling salted water and cook in their skins until just tender – about 15 minutes. Drain, then shake in the pan over the heat for a moment to dry. Tip into a large bowl. Trim the onions and chop all the white part and some of the green stems. Whisk together the mustard, vinegar and oil and season well. Pour over the potatoes and coat. Add the onions. Leave to cool for at least 1 hour – this is best not refrigerated. Stir in the herbs.

Raspberry and pecan muffins

Find pretty splashes of red raspberry when you break the muffins open.

275 g (10 oz) plain flour
3 teaspoons baking powder
½ teaspoon salt
75 g (3 oz) unrefined golden
  caster sugar
50 g (2 oz) chopped pecans
1 egg
300 ml (10 fl oz) milk
75 ml (3 fl oz) grapeseed or
  other light oil
100 g (4 oz) fresh raspberries

For the cinnamon sugar

50 g (2 oz) unrefined golden
  caster sugar
½ teaspoon ground cinnamon

Heat the oven to 200°C/400°F/Gas Mark 6. Generously oil a 12-cup muffin or deep bun tray or drop in muffin paper cups. Sift the flour, baking powder and salt into a large bowl. Add the sugar and pecans and mix. Crack the egg into a smaller bowl, add the milk and oil. Mix with a fork. Add the liquid mixture to the dry ingredients all at once and stir with a large spoon until the ingredients are moist – don't over-blend, the mixture should be lumpy. Lightly stir in the raspberries. Spoon into the muffin tray, filling each one two-thirds full. Sprinkle with a little mixed sugar and cinnamon for a crunchy crust.

Bake for 15–20 minutes or until well risen. Allow to cool for 2 minutes, then loosen (unless you're using paper cups) and turn muffins on to a wire cooling rack.

Wine recommendations

A summer-fresh white with good aromatic personality would work wonders with this picnic spread, and there is no finer example of this style than Alsace Gewürztraminer, with its violet-tinged bouquet and its fat, rich, positively oily texture. If you're determined to drink a red, bear in mind that the lazy days of summer are where Beaujolais comes into its own, and something like a Fleurie or a Chiroubles would be particularly appetizing with the duck. Put it in the chiller-bag too, as the lower temperature will help to bring out its exhilarating strawberry fruit. The muffins don't necessarily require another wine, but a tot of something like late-harvest Muscat from America wouldn't go amiss.

THE SOPHISTICATED PICNIC

menu for 6

- TARAMASALATA ON RYE BREAD
- ITALIAN-STYLE FRESH TUNA SALAD
- RAVIOLI SALAD WITH PESTO DRESSING
- GREEN SALAD WITH GREEN BEANS
- BROWN SUGAR MERINGUES WITH FRESH RASPBERRIES

There's a lovely summer tradition gaining ground of taking meals to eat at an open-air concert or play – where I live the annual treat is Shakespeare in the park. We make quite an occasion of it, taking along china and cutlery, folding tables and chairs and various dishes in bowls ready to serve. Sitting at a little table means you can use a knife and fork, which makes it much easier to plan the menu.

Start with home-made taramasalata served on rye bread – it's ideal finger food, so pass it round with a glass of wine while everyone is settling down. Chargrilled fresh tuna and summer vegetables make a substantial salad; this version has an Italian twist. Small slices of tuna will chargrill in minutes but you can use well-drained

and flaked canned tuna instead. Stir in a dressing, then add colour with hard-boiled eggs, green capers, shiny black olives and a sprinkling of chopped parsley. Using spinach and ricotta-filled ravioli to make a pasta salad is a brilliant idea. Filled pasta shapes are attractive plump pillows, and when served with a basil and parsley dressing make a delicious second dish. With these two you don't need much more than a simple combination of green salad leaves and green beans cooked *al dente*, with a drizzle of olive oil added on site.

Home-made brown sugar meringues always go down well. Serve them with a big bowl of raspberries and cream. If the raspberries are freshly picked they will be even more delicious.

The day before
Make brown sugar meringues. Prepare taramasalata and refrigerate covered with cling film.

Early on the day
Cook spinach and ricotta ravioli and prepare dressing separately. Cook green beans, rinse and crisp up salad leaves (see Katie's tip). Prepare Italian-style fresh tuna salad, cover with cling film and refrigerate. Pick over raspberries – do not chill.

I hour before
Take tuna salad from refrigerator. Mix and turn spinach and ricotta ravioli with pesto dressing.

Last minute
Toss green salad with green beans. Check you have rye bread and cream for dessert.

Taramasalata on rye bread

When taramasalata is home-made the result is paler, finer tasting and altogether more delicious than the shop-bought variety.

*250 g (9 oz) smoked
  cod's roe
200 ml (7 fl oz) olive oil
1 thick slice white bread
1 clove garlic
Juice 1 large lemon
Freshly milled pepper
Slices of rye bread for serving*

With a vegetable knife tip, score the skin of the cod's roe in several places and put in a mixing bowl. Pour over boiling water to cover and let the roe stand for 2–3 minutes to loosen the skin. Drain and, while warm, peel off as much of the skin as possible. Cut the roe in pieces, put in a bowl with 2 tablespoons of the measured olive oil and leave to soften for 15 minutes.

Meanwhile trim the crusts from the bread slice and soak the bread in 3–4 tablespoons of cold water for a few minutes. Then squeeze the bread dry – it should be soft and pulpy. Peel the garlic and crush to a purée. Press the cod's roe and oil from the bowl through a sieve, to remove any last little pieces of skin – discard anything remaining in the sieve. Place the roe in a mixing bowl or food processor bowl. Add the soaked bread, garlic and lemon juice.

At this stage use either an electric hand mixer or food processor for blending. Whiz the ingredients to a purée. With the motor still running, pour in the rest of the oil (through the feed tube on a processor) until the mixture has the consistency of mayonnaise. Taste and season with milled pepper. Turn the mixture into a serving bowl and let it mature for 1 hour or longer before serving with rye bread. The taramasalata will keep for up to 1 week in the refrigerator.

Italian-style fresh tuna salad

This is one of those salads where you layer all the elements, and then stir it up just before serving to mix the contents.

500 g (1 lb 2 oz) fresh tuna, cut in thick pieces or steaks
7–9 tablespoons olive oil
2 teaspoons cracked black pepper
1–2 lemons for squeezing
6 eggs
750 g (1¾ lb) new potatoes
1 small onion
1 tablespoon balsamic vinegar
Salt and freshly milled pepper
3 sticks celery
3–4 tablespoons salted capers
3 tablespoons chopped flatleaf parsley
8–10 black olives

Cut the tuna steaks into thin slanting slices. Turn both sides in 2–3 tablespoons of olive oil and the cracked pepper. Heat a ridged grill pan until quite hot, put 4–5 tuna pieces on at a time and cook for about 1 minute, turning once. The tuna should be not quite cooked through – a little pink in the middle is best. Transfer the grilled pieces of tuna to a plate as you add the next batch to the pan. Squeeze the lemon juice over the tuna and allow to cool.

Put the eggs in a pan with cold water to cover, bring to a simmer and cook for 6 minutes to hard-boil, drain at once and plunge into cold water. Shell the eggs. Rinse the potatoes – there's no need to scrub or scrape. Add them to a pan of boiling salted water and simmer for 10–15 minutes until tender. Drain, and turn on to a clean tea cloth to dry. Cut the hot potatoes into thick slices and turn into a mixing bowl. Add the peeled, halved and finely sliced onion. Add 5–6 tablespoons of olive oil, the balsamic vinegar and a good seasoning of salt and pepper. Stir up the potatoes with a fork and let stand for at least an hour to absorb the flavour.

Trim the celery sticks and string them, then cut lengthways and across to finely chop. Add the celery to the potato mixture and stir through. Turn the potato mixture into a serving bowl. Spoon the grilled tuna on top, add the hard-boiled eggs, quartered, then the capers – rinsed under the cold tap to remove the salt – a generous sprinkling of chopped parsley and finally a scattering of black olives.

Ravioli salad with pesto dressing

All pasta salads are best when freshly cooked and mixed. Stir through the basil-flavoured pesto dressing and parsley shortly before you set out.

500 g (1 lb 2 oz) fresh spinach and ricotta ravioli
3 tablespoons olive oil for the pasta

For the pesto dressing
100 ml (3½ fl oz) olive oil
2 tablespoons white wine vinegar
Juice 1 lemon
1 clove garlic, crushed
3 tablespoons prepared pesto sauce
Salt and freshly milled pepper
2 tablespoons finely chopped flatleaf parsley

Cook the ravioli according to the packet directions, or add to a large pan of boiling salted water with 1 tablespoon of olive oil and simmer gently for 4 minutes. Drain the ravioli well and turn into a large bowl. Add 2 tablespoons of olive oil and mix gently to coat the pasta and prevent it from sticking. Let the pasta cool but do not chill.

In a bowl combine the olive oil for the dressing, the vinegar, lemon juice, crushed garlic, pesto sauce and a seasoning of salt and freshly milled pepper. Add the pesto dressing to the ravioli and, using a fork, mix through gently. Add an extra seasoning of milled pepper and the chopped parsley and mix again. Spoon the salad on to a serving platter.

Green salad with green beans

A pretty and very simple salad combination, this is often found on the menu at French restaurants. The beans are served *al dente*.

200 g (7 oz) fine green beans
2 baby Cos or 3 Little Gem lettuces
Extra-virgin olive oil
Salt and freshly milled pepper

Trim the green beans at the stalk end but leave them whole with tails intact. Add to a pan of boiling salted water and cook for 6 minutes until tender, then drain and immediately plunge into a bowl of cold water to preserve the bright green colour. When the beans have cooled down, drain and shake off all water droplets.

Separate the lettuce leaves, tear them into smaller pieces and turn them into a salad bowl. Scatter the beans on top. Drizzle with extra-virgin olive oil and season with salt and freshly milled pepper.

Katie's tip

Salad greens will crisp up beautifully in the refrigerator and you can get them ready ahead. Separate and rinse the leaves, then shake them dry either in a tea towel or in a salad spinner; you must remove all the water droplets because wet leaves will turn brown. Enclose the leaves in a roomy polythene bag and tie closed. The contents can be a mixture of leaves ready to serve, if you like. Put them low down in the refrigerator where they will keep fresh for up to 48 hours. Herbs also take well to this treatment; chill them in a closed bag to keep them fresh and flavoursome.

Brown sugar meringues with fresh raspberries

I always use unrefined demerara sugar for brown sugar meringues as it gives them a wonderful taste and a perfect, pale golden colour.

100 g (4 oz) unrefined demerara or golden caster sugar
2 egg whites
500 g (1 lb 2 oz) fresh raspberries
300 ml (10 fl oz) single cream, to serve

Heat the oven to 140°C/275°F/Gas Mark 1. Cut two sheets of non-stick baking parchment to fit two baking trays and line the trays. It helps if you dry the sugar for these meringues in a low oven – unrefined sugars are often quite damp. Spread the sugar on a sheet of greaseproof paper on a baking tray and set in the oven to dry for 20 minutes. Then, if demerara sugar is your choice, buzz in the blender for a finer texture.

Whisk the egg whites to stiff peaks. Add half the sugar, 1 tablespoon at a time, and whisk in each addition well, whisking until the meringue is stiff and glossy. Sprinkle the remaining sugar over the beaten meringue and gently fold in, using the cutting edge of a tablespoon – the mixture should retain its volume.

Scoop out dessertspoonfuls of the mixture and drop them on to the lined tray – you should get 12 meringues. Keep the spoonfuls rough-looking – not too neat – so everyone knows they are home-made and taste the nicer for it. Cook the meringues in the heated oven for a minimum of 2–3 hours, until they slide off the tray easily. When they're cold, enclose them in tightly tied polythene bags to keep them dry. Pick over the raspberries and pile in a bowl. Offer brown sugar meringues, raspberries and cream separately and let guests help themselves to what they want.

Wine recommendations

White wines all the way are what's needed with this picnic spread. High acidity will be best with the oily taramasalata, so go for Muscadet de Sèvre-et-Maine, or one of the dry Chenin wines from further along the Loire Valley, such as Vouvray or Montlouis, or even a crisp young Chablis. Something a little richer and creamier might be better with the salads, though, so carry on further east until you arrive in Burgundy. Youthful Rully or Montagny with just a touch of oak will answer the call. Failing that, you could choose a tropically scented unoaked Chardonnay from Chile or New Zealand, but avoid anything too heavily oaked. I'd be inclined to enjoy the meringue and raspberries just as they are, without the need for another wine.

TABLE UNDER
THE TREES

menu for 10

- MIXED BROCHETTES

  Pork satays

  Halloumi brochettes

  Skewered potatoes

  Tiger prawns with chilli aioli

- SAFFRON RICE PILAFF

- MIXED LEAF SALAD

- HOT GARLIC BREAD

- VANILLA PANNA COTTA WITH
  POACHED FRUITS

You can't beat a barbecue on a sunny summer's day. Whether yours is traditional charcoal, smart gas-fired or a series of smaller portable, disposable ones, get it alight for a weekend lunch party. You can be flexible about when guests arrive as my choice of menu means the food can be cooked to order and ready in minutes.

Small items like brochettes are ideal – you can pop them over the heat as you need them for serving. Marinate foods overnight, then slide them on to bamboo skewers ahead of time and return them to the refrigerator until cooking time. You will find that it's easier to marinate pieces in freezer bags, which will take up less space than a bowl (but use proper freezer bags and tie them tightly so they don't leak). There are sufficient brochettes here for guests to have some of everything,

or they can concentrate on just one or two, if they prefer. Hand round dipping sauces such as soured cream with chives, flavoured mayonnaise and fresh vegetable relishes. Serve the brochettes with a delicious rice pilaff – a hot rice dish always goes well with barbecued foods. Add a mixed leaf salad; use small leaves such as rocket, watercress, salad spinach, baby red chard, mizuna and fresh herbs, seasoned and drizzled with olive oil. My garlic bread is particularly good and crunchy and made a different way. Let your guests tuck into it with a glass of chilled wine as they arrive.

For the finale of this summer lunch party, I've chosen little panna cottas. They're delicious vanilla-flavoured puddings, perfect served with poached fruits – nectarines, apricots or plums would be my choice.

timeplan

The day before

Make, mould and chill panna cottas; poach fruit. Marinate ingredients for pork, prawn and halloumi brochettes and refrigerate. Make chilli aioli. Prepare garlic bread, cover and chill.

Early on the day

Cook potatoes and marinate. Cook, blanch and cut up mangetout for pilaff. Prepare leaves for mixed salad and refrigerate. Soak bamboo skewers for brochettes and they will be less likely to scorch.

1 hour before

Skewer all brochettes ready for cooking, and refrigerate. Assemble ingredients for saffron rice pilaff. Light barbecue.

About 30 minutes before

Put saffron rice pilaff to cook.

Mixed brochettes

Marinated brochettes are ideal for barbecues – they are simple to prepare and cook quickly. Pork satays and skewered tiger prawns are sure to be popular, while halloumi cheese brochettes and skewered potatoes make a satisfying vegetarian alternative.

Pork satays

2 pork tenderloins, about
  400 g (14 oz) each

For the marinade
3 tablespoons soft brown sugar
4 tablespoons dark soy sauce
6 tablespoons vegetable oil
Juice 1 large lemon
2–3 cloves crushed garlic
5 cm (2 in) fresh ginger, grated

With a sharp knife strip away any sinew from the pork fillets. Slice the fillets thinly against the grain, holding the knife at an angle – like slicing smoked salmon. From each pork fillet you should get about 20 slices.

Measure the ingredients for the marinade into a bowl or large freezer bag. Add the pork pieces and turn them to coat. Cover (or tie the freezer bag tightly) and refrigerate for 4 hours or overnight. Crinkle three pieces of meat, reasonably close together, on each of 10–12 wooden skewers. Refrigerate until cooking time.

Halloumi brochettes

2 x 250 g pack halloumi
  cheese
500 g (1 lb 2 oz) ripe cherry
  tomatoes
4–6 tablespoons olive oil
Freshly milled black pepper

Remove halloumi cheese from the wrapping and blot up any liquid with kitchen paper. Cut the cheese into cubes of about 2.5 cm (1 in). In a bowl (or large freezer bag) combine the cheese, tomatoes, oil and milled pepper. Cover (or tie the bag tightly), and refrigerate for 4 hours or overnight. Thread tomatoes and halloumi on to each of 10–12 wooden skewers. Refrigerate until cooking time.

Skewered potatoes

1 kg (2¼ lb) small new
  potatoes
5–6 tablespoons olive oil
2–3 cloves garlic
Sea salt and black pepper

Rinse or scrub new potatoes; cut larger ones in half. Add to boiling salted water and simmer for 10–12 minutes or until knife-tip tender. Drain and turn the hot potatoes into a bowl, add the oil and garlic, peeled and flattened with a knife blade. Let the potatoes cool, then cover and marinate for up to 4 hours. Slide 3–4 potatoes on to each of 10–12 wooden skewers. Season the potatoes with salt and milled black pepper. Keep cool, but not chilled, until cooking time.

Mixed brochettes (continued)

Tiger prawns with chilli aioli

700 g (1½ lb) raw, peeled
* tiger prawns*

For the marinade

6 tablespoons vegetable oil
3 tablespoons sweet chilli
* sauce*
1 tablespoon Thai fish sauce
Juice 1 large lemon
Freshly milled black pepper

For the chilli aioli

300 ml (10 fl oz) mayon-
* naise*
2–3 teaspoons fresh hot chilli
* in sunflower oil or chilli*
* sauce*
2 cloves garlic
1 tablespoon soft brown sugar
Salt and freshly milled black
* pepper*

If prawns are frozen, allow to thaw and drain off any liquid. In a bowl (or large freezer bag) combine the ingredients for the marinade. Mix well and taste – it should be spicy. Add the prawns, cover (or tie the bag tightly) and refrigerate for 4 hours or overnight. Combine ingredients for the aioli and chill.

Scoop the prawns from the marinade and thread up to 5 on each of the 10 wooden skewers. Skewer through the body and tail end to hold in shape. Refrigerate until cooking time.

Cooking the brochettes

When the barbecue is hot, set a selection of mixed brochettes to cook. Turn them once to cook both sides. Allow 5–6 minutes for pork satays; 3–4 minutes for the prawns – they will turn from grey to red. For the halloumi cheese allow 5 minutes; and for the potatoes 4–5 minutes. Serve as soon as they're cooked, allowing 2–3 brochettes per person.

Saffron rice pilaff

Any kind of hot rice dish will team up perfectly with barbecue foods.

1 litre (1¾ pints) vegetable
  stock
½ –1 teaspoon saffron strands
2 medium onions
3 tablespoons olive oil
500 g (1 lb 2 oz) long
  grain rice
300 g (11 oz) mangetout
50 g (2 oz) butter
100 g (4 oz) toasted, flaked
  almonds
2–3 tablespoons chopped
  flatleaf parsley
Freshly milled black pepper

Make up the vegetable stock – I would use Marigold vegetable bouillon powder. Gently crumble the saffron strands with your fingers and stir into the hot stock. Peel and finely chop the onions. Heat the oil in a pan, stir in the onion and soften over a moderate heat.

Add the rice, stir into the oil and onions and cook for a few moments more. Add the stock and stir as it comes to the boil. Cover and simmer over a low heat for 15–20 minutes or until the liquid is absorbed.

Trim the mangetout and steam or boil for 3–4 minutes – they should be tender yet crisp. Immediately plunge the mangetout into a bowl of cold water to fix the green colour, then drain well. With a sharp knife cut the mangetout into diagonal slivers – these look prettier in the rice. When the rice is cooked, draw the pan off the heat, add the mangetout and the butter, re-cover with the pan lid and leave for 10 minutes. Add the almonds, parsley and a seasoning of pepper. With a fork gently turn the mixture. Turn on to a roomy serving dish.

Hot garlic bread

Make plenty – this is delicious!

225 g (8 oz) unsalted butter
6 cloves garlic
½ teaspoon salt
4 tablespoons olive oil
4–5 tablespoons chopped
  parsley
Freshly milled black pepper
2 long baguettes

Measure the butter into a food processor bowl, then peel the garlic cloves and mash with the salt. Add the oil and garlic to the butter and mix to a soft blend. Add the parsley and pepper and mix using the on/off or pulse switch. Cut each baguette in half so you have four pieces. Then cut each half horizontally to make 8 pieces. Spread each cut side with the garlic butter. Cover and chill until just before serving time.

Heat the oven to 190°C/375°F/Gas Mark 5. Bake for 15–20 minutes. Cut across in chunks for serving: makes 32 pieces.

Vanilla panna cotta with poached fruits

The flavoursome black seeds from real vanilla pods will speckle the surface of these delicious little puddings.

5 leaves gelatine
600 ml (1 pint) double cream
2 vanilla pods
100 g (4 oz) caster sugar
600 ml (1 pint) single cream

For the fruit

300 ml (10 fl oz) red or rosé
wine
175 g (6 oz) caster sugar
1 piece stick cinnamon
Pared zest and juice of
1 lemon
12 nectarines, plums or
apricots

Select 10 small moulds – I use dariole moulds – each holding just under 100 ml (3½ fl oz). Rinse with cold water and set close together on a flat tray that will fit in the refrigerator. Put the gelatine in a bowl – cut the leaves in half if it helps. Cover with cold water and let the leaves soak for 5 minutes. Meanwhile measure the double cream into a pan. Split the vanilla pods in half and scrape out the black seeds – add the seeds to the cream.

Bring the double cream almost to the boil and draw off the heat. Pick the gelatine leaves out of the cold water, and squeeze them to remove the water. Add them to the hot cream, stir and the gelatine will dissolve immediately. Stir in the sugar and, when this has dissolved, stir in the single cream. Pour the mixture into each mould, filling it level. Cool, then carefully transfer moulds to the refrigerator and chill for 4 hours or overnight until set firm.

Measure the wine, sugar and 300 ml (10 fl oz) water into a large pan. Add the cinnamon and lemon zest. Stir until the sugar has dissolved, then bring to the boil and draw off the heat. Cut around each fruit following the natural line from the stalk end. Twist the halves in opposite directions to remove the stone. Add to the syrup. Simmer gently for 6–8 minutes or until tender. With a perforated spoon, transfer the fruits to a serving bowl. Discard the lemon zest and cinnamon, add the lemon juice and pour the syrup over the fruits. Cool, then chill for up to 4 hours or overnight.

To serve, unmould each panna cotta and offer with the poached fruits and syrup.

Wine recommendations

Mix and match between white and rosé wines to suit the summer mood of this menu. A pink wine from the south of France or one of the fruity Grenache or Shiraz rosés from Australia will measure up to both the seafood and the brochettes. A white wine will need to be richly textured to suit these dishes: choose a buttery Chardonnay or an oaked Sémillon from California, South Africa or Australia. Alternatively, one of the wood-matured Chardonnays from Hungary or Bulgaria would fit the bill. A lightly botrytized (see page 18) wine from Germany, Austria or somewhere like Monbazillac in south-west France would be a tasty match for panna cotta.

Party Parties

A TASTE OF ITALY

menu for 12

- HERB-MARINATED LAMB SKEWERS
- GRILLED MARINATED SWEET PEPPERS
- RICOTTA AND SPINACH PASTA SHELLS
- FENNEL SALAD WITH ROCKET AND PARMESAN
- GARLIC CIABATTA BREAD
- LEMON POLENTA CAKE

It's a fun idea to give a buffet menu a theme – this one is Italian-style with hot main dishes. I've teamed one easy-to-assemble, prepare-ahead pasta bake with a simple dish of fresh, herb-marinated lamb on skewers. Go to town on salads, using colourful Mediterranean ingredients; my marinated red and yellow peppers are sweet tasting, and the salad of grilled fennel and fresh rocket with Parmesan shavings is a feast of flavours.

Make this occasion an excuse to visit a good Italian deli to buy the larger pasta shells for stuffing, a chunk of Parmesan – the flavour is always better when taken from a big piece – and classy extra-virgin olive oil for salads and hot breads. Concentrate on the flavours here; use

timeplan

The day before

Assemble pasta shells
with ricotta and spinach
filling and tomato ragu.
Cover and refrigerate.
Prepare grilled marinated
peppers and keep cool.
Bake lemon polenta cake.

In the morning

Marinate lamb pieces.
Grill fennel and prepare
ingredients for fennel salad
with rocket and Parmesan.

1–2 hours before

Thread lamb pieces on
to skewers and arrange
on trays.

30 minutes before

Put pasta shells in tomato
ragu to reheat. Grill or
oven-cook lamb skewers.
Place garlic heads to bake
(along with lamb skewers
in the oven), and lastly
ciabatta bread. Combine
and toss ingredients for
fennel salad.

black pepper ground from a mill and sea salt flakes when seasoning salad – this is important when the dressing is just a good olive oil. Nutmeg also has a wonderful flavour and is a must for pasta dishes, particularly those that include spinach. Buy one or two whole nutmegs as it's best freshly grated – I use the fine holes on my box-shaped grater. With the fresh herbs – thyme sprigs, mint or oregano – use the leaves stripped off the stems.

Lastly, the lemon polenta cake is truly delicious. I think it tastes best warm so, if you get the chance, wrap the baked cake in foil and pop it into a hot oven for about 10 minutes, then serve in slices with spoonfuls of chilled mascarpone.

Herb-marinated lamb skewers

Marinated lamb is always delicious. For this recipe you need a tender, lean cut and my choice is a leg of lamb because so little needs to be trimmed off. Serve the lamb skewers as they do in the Mediterranean countries – with lemon wedges for squeezing over them.

1 boned leg of lamb or 1.5 kg (3 lb) lean lamb pieces
5–6 tablespoons olive oil
Grated zest and juice 1 lemon
2 teaspoons dried oregano
3–4 cloves garlic, peeled and crushed
Freshly milled pepper
4 tablespoons chopped fresh mint or oregano
4–6 lemons for serving

Trim the lamb and cut into bite-sized pieces. Measure the oil, lemon zest and juice, and dried oregano into a mixing bowl. Add the crushed garlic, milled pepper and chopped fresh herb, followed by the pieces of meat; turn to coat them with the marinade. Cover and leave to marinate in the refrigerator for at least 4 hours, tossing occasionally with a fork. Thread the lamb pieces on to 12 bamboo skewers, allowing 3–4 pieces for each one. Arrange the lamb skewers on foil-lined baking trays.

Place the lamb skewers under a heated grill to cook for 15 minutes, turning once. As an easier, more convenient method, push the trays of lamb into an oven heated to 200°C/400°F/Gas Mark 6, and cook for about the same time – turn so that the meat browns on both sides. Serve with lemon wedges.

Grilled marinated sweet peppers

Grilling red and yellow peppers brings out their natural sweetness.

8 sweet peppers – red and yellow
1 large onion
6–8 tablespoons olive oil
2 teaspoons caster sugar
1 tablespoon fresh thyme leaves
Salt and freshly milled pepper
Juice 1 lemon

Heat the grill to hot and set the grill pan about 7.5 cm (3 in) from the heat. Quarter the peppers lengthways and remove the seeds. Crowd the pepper pieces on one or more baking trays, skin-side-up, and grill until the skins are blistered and charred. Cover the hot peppers and tray with a cloth and leave for about 10 minutes, until they're cool enough to handle. Peel off the charred skins, and place the pepper pieces in a serving dish.

Peel, halve and thinly slice the onion. Heat 2 tablespoons of olive oil in a frying-pan, add the onion and sprinkle with the sugar. Cook gently until the onion is softened and turning golden,

then sprinkle in the thyme and stir. Add salt and plenty of milled pepper, and the remaining oil and lemon juice. Bring to a simmer and pour over the peppers. Marinate for up to 6 hours, or overnight, in a cool place – preferably not the refrigerator.

Ricotta and spinach pasta shells

An Italian deli or specialist food shop will stock large pasta shells.

*25–30 large pasta shells
(conchiglie)*
*900 g (2 lb) fresh spinach or
500 g (1 lb 2 oz) frozen,
chopped spinach*
3 x 250 g tubs ricotta
Salt and freshly milled pepper
Grated nutmeg
*1.5 kg (3 lb) ripe plum
tomatoes*
3–4 cloves garlic
2 tablespoons olive oil
*1 tablespoon fresh thyme
leaves*
*4 tablespoons grated
Parmesan*

Add the large pasta shells to a pan of boiling salted water, stir as the water reboils and cook for 10 minutes until the shells are barely tender. Drain, then plunge the pasta shells into a bowl of cold water to cool. Pull away the spinach stalks and wash the leaves in cold water, then pack them in a pan and cook for 1–2 minutes, until wilted. Drain and press the spinach well to extract the moisture, then chop coarsely. If using frozen, chopped spinach, allow it to thaw in a colander and discard the liquid.

Turn the ricotta into a mixing bowl. Season with salt and milled pepper and a generous grating of fresh nutmeg. Add the chopped spinach and mix. Stuff each pasta shell with a tablespoon of the ricotta and spinach mixture, and then arrange the filled shells in roomy, oiled 1.75 litre (3 pint) baking dishes – try to keep the shells in a single layer (you'll need at least two dishes).

Cut out and discard the stalk ends from the tomatoes, then cut the tomatoes coarsely. Peel and finely chop or crush the garlic. Warm the olive oil in a large pan, add the garlic and heat for a moment, so that the oil takes the flavour of the garlic. Add the tomatoes, thyme leaves and seasoning, then let the mixture simmer for 15–20 minutes or until a thick ragu has formed. Spoon the ragu over the filled pasta shells. Up to this stage you can prepare the recipe in advance – but refrigerate no longer than overnight.

Heat the oven to 180°C/350°F/Gas Mark 4. Sprinkle the pasta shells with the grated Parmesan, set in the heated oven and bake for 20–25 minutes, or until bubbling hot – it will take longer if the dishes are still cold from the refrigerator – and then serve.

Fennel salad with rocket and Parmesan

This is a very pretty salad, so keep the dressing simple – extra-virgin olive oil with sea salt and milled pepper.

5 fennel bulbs
6 tablespoons olive oil for grilling
4 heads chicory
200 g (7 oz) rocket leaves
75 g (3 oz) toasted pine kernels
100 g (4 oz) piece Parmesan
4–6 tablespoons extra-virgin olive oil
Sea salt and freshly milled pepper

Snip the feathery bits from the fennel and discard, otherwise keep the bulbs whole. Add them to a pan of boiling water, return to the boil, then simmer for 5–6 minutes to tenderize. Drain, cool and pat dry. Halve the bulbs lengthways, place the cut sides to the chopping board and slice lengthways again – giving about 4 from each half bulb.

Spread the fennel slices on to baking trays in one layer. Brush with oil and pass under a hot grill, turning once and brushing with more oil until the slices are brown-tinged and soft – this will take about 8 minutes.

Slice the chicory heads in half and cut out the core. Then cut across the leaves in slices 2.5 cm (1 in) thick and separate the leaves. In a salad bowl combine the grilled fennel, trimmed chicory, rocket leaves and pine kernels. Just before serving, scatter Parmesan shavings (use a vegetable peeler) and toss with extra-virgin olive oil, sea salt and milled pepper.

Garlic ciabatta bread

Serve hot and crunchy for guests to spread with soft, roasted garlic.

4–6 whole garlic heads
4–6 plain ciabatta loaves
Extra-virgin olive oil

Heat the oven to 200°C/400°F/Gas Mark 6. Take a slice from the tops of the garlic heads – to reveal the cloves within – and roast for 35–40 minutes. Meanwhile, split the ciabatta loaves in half lengthways. Place the loaves cut sides up on baking trays. Drizzle the bread surfaces generously with the olive oil. Slide them into the hot oven and bake for 15–20 minutes until golden and crunchy. Slice the loaves across and serve with the roasted garlic ready for spreading.

Lemon polenta cake

An unusual, lemony-flavoured treat, based on a recipe from Ursula Ferrigno's *Ursula's Italian Cakes and Desserts* (Metro Books).

175 g (6 oz) ground almonds
100 g (4 oz) instant polenta
1 teaspoon baking powder
¼ teaspoon salt
275 g (10 oz) butter
275 g (10 oz) caster sugar
Juice 4 large lemons
6 eggs
Icing sugar for dusting
500 g (1 lb 2 oz)
   mascarpone, to serve

Heat the oven to 180°C/350°F/Gas Mark 4. Well butter and base line a 23 cm (9 in) spring-clip baking tin, then dust with flour. Combine the ground almonds, polenta, baking powder and salt and mix well. Turn the mixture on to a sheet of greaseproof paper.

In a mixing bowl, cream the butter, sugar and finely grated lemon zest until soft and light. Separate the eggs, beating the yolks into the mixture one at a time. Add the ground almond and polenta mixture, and stir in the lemon juice. Whisk the egg whites to soft peaks and fold into the mix with a tablespoon. Turn into the prepared tin and spread level.

Bake in the heated oven for 45–50 minutes. Unclip the sides of the tin, loosen and remove the polenta cake when it's cold. Dust with the icing sugar and serve slices with mascarpone.

Wine recommendations

It would be unthinkable to serve anything other than Italian wines with this menu, and there are many more good ones about now than there used to be. A silky-textured white wine such as Arneis from Piedmont or good Soave Classico from the Veneto would each be well-suited to the pasta dish, or there are fine, savoury lightly oaked Chardonnays now from regions like Umbria. With the lamb, though, a red is called for. Montepulciano d'Abruzzo from the east or Salice Salentino from Puglia are both widely available reds with gentle tannins and plenty of ripe plum fruit on the palate. Look for the delicious sweet wine, vin santo, to serve with the lemon cake. It's made from raisined grapes, is rich and citric, and has just the right weight to stand up to the cake's consistency.

CELEBRATION SUPPER

menu for 12

- SEARED SALMON IN MUSTARD AND DILL

- BULGAR SALAD WITH FRUIT AND NUTS

- COURGETTE AND TARRAGON MOULDS

- VEGETABLE SALAD WITH HONEY DRESSING

- NUTMEG ICE-CREAM

I like party menus to contain a few surprises. It's fun to give guests a taste of something different, so the emphasis here is on intriguing flavour combinations. Seared salmon in individual portions, served cold with a mustard and dill dressing (salmon copes well with strong flavours) gets neatly around the problem of serving a crowd quickly. The alternative would be to serve the salmon portions with a mustard mayonnaise; just stir Dijon mustard into mayonnaise to taste – so simple yet superb.

A vegetable recipe is a good idea for a second main dish. You won't need many of my pretty courgette and tarragon moulds because most guests will go for the salmon, but offering an alternative caters for all tastes. Having said that, I find guests tend to try everything – so you can always slice the moulds in half and the whole lot

timeplan

The day before

Make nutmeg ice-cream –
twice. Prepare and bake
courgette and tarragon
moulds. Make bulgar salad
with fruit and marinate.
Toast almonds for bulgar
salad and set aside.

In the morning

Prepare seared salmon and
dressing and refrigerate.
Make vegetable salad and
honey dressing but keep
them separate.

I hour before

Toss vegetable salad
with honey dressing. Stir
toasted almonds into
bulgar salad.

will probably be happily polished off! Salads for this menu
should be adventurous too, such as bulgar wheat with
fruit and nuts – the lemon juice makes it fresh tasting –
and seasonal summer vegetables combined together in a
big salad bowl with a honey-flavoured dressing.

For real home-made ice-cream, start with a custard-
based recipe; I've added grated nutmeg so this recipe
comes up creamy-coloured with a wonderful scented
flavour. Serve it in style – as scoops in small glass
tumblers, or in smart espresso cups set on saucers. Have
glasses or coffee cups well chilled and use a small-sized
ice-cream scoop. Add a sprinkle of light muscovado sugar
for decoration – it's pretty when the sugar dissolves a bit
– and into each serving tuck a *Langue du chat*, a *Cigarette
russe* or any other sweet biscuit that takes your fancy.

Seared salmon in mustard and dill

Salmon prepared this way allows individual servings to be taken easily.

2 kg (4½ lb) salmon, either
    two long fillets or 12 thick-
    cut salmon fillet portions,
    all with skin on
Sea salt and milled pepper
Olive oil
2–3 lemons for serving

For the dressing

1 tablespoon grainy mustard
1 teaspoon Dijon mustard
1 teaspoon light muscovado
    sugar
2 tablespoons white wine
    vinegar
6 tablespoons olive oil
2 tablespoons grapeseed or
    other light oil
Salt and freshly milled pepper
2 tablespoons chopped dill

With a sharp knife, trim the narrow edges on the belly side of the fillets. Run your fingers across the flesh and tweeze out any tiny bones – mostly around the head end. Cut each fillet across into 6 portions. Season the flesh side of the portions with sea salt and coarsely milled pepper.

Heat the grill to hot and set the grill rack 7.5 cm (3 in) from the heat source. Brush 2 baking trays with olive oil and arrange the salmon portions on them, skin-side-up. Slide the trays, one at a time, under the grill and grill the fillets for 8–10 minutes. Do not turn the fish pieces; cook from one side only, allowing the skin to brown and crinkle. Cool, then refrigerate.

For the dressing, combine both mustards, the sugar, vinegar, olive and grapeseed oil and a seasoning of salt and milled pepper. Stir well to mix, then stir in the dill and refrigerate alongside the salmon.

Take the lemons and cut a slice through to the flesh from each of the ends. Then cut the lemon skin in quarters (as if peeling an orange). Place the lemons in a bowl and pour over boiling water to cover. Stand for 5 minutes. Drain and pull off the lemon peels – as the lemons are warm the peel will come away easily. Slice the peeled lemons and discard any pips.

Transfer the salmon to serving platters. Scatter with the lemon slices and drizzle over the dressing.

Bulgar salad with fruit and nuts

Use couscous in exactly the same way as the bulgar if you prefer.

*200 g (7 oz) 'ready to eat'
    dried apricots*
*100 ml (3½ fl oz) fresh
    orange juice*
*500 g (1 lb 2 oz) bulgar
    wheat*
*600 ml (1 pint) vegetable
    stock*
3 tablespoons olive oil
3 bunches spring onions
Grated rind 1 lemon
Juice 2 lemons
Salt and freshly milled pepper
*100 g (4 oz) whole skinned
    almonds*

Snip the apricots into slivers. Add to the orange juice in a bowl
and soak for 1 hour or until the apricots are soft. Measure the
bulgar into a large bowl. Bring the vegetable stock to the boil.
Pour over the bulgar, then cover the bowl with a cloth. Leave to
stand until the liquid is absorbed – about 20–30 minutes. Mix in
the olive oil and cool.   *couscous doesn't take as long
(10 min)*

Wash and trim the spring onions, then chop the white part
and some of the stems. Add to the bulgar along with the apricots
and orange juice. Add the rind and juice of the lemons and a
seasoning of salt and milled pepper. Refrigerate and let the salad
marinate for at least 2 hours. Cut the skinned almonds lengthways
into slivers – if they're dry or brittle, cover with boiling water
for 5 minutes to soften, then drain and slice. Toast them in a hot
oven or under the grill until golden, then add to the salad.

Courgette and tarragon moulds

Offer with Parma ham to serve – the flavours are excellent together.

500 g (1 lb 2 oz) small,
  tender courgettes
1 medium onion
6–8 sprigs fresh tarragon
2 tablespoons olive oil
1 x 250 g tub ricotta
2 eggs
50 g (2 oz) fresh white
  breadcrumbs
Salt and freshly milled pepper
25 g (1 oz) grated Parmesan
6 tablespoons prepared oil and
  vinegar dressing
Tarragon leaves to garnish
Parma ham (optional)

Heat the oven to 180°C/350°F/Gas Mark 4. Lightly oil six 150 ml (5 fl oz) pudding moulds. Wash and trim the courgettes. Using a swivel peeler, take strips of the skin from the length of 1 or 2 courgettes – you need 2 strips for each mould. Put the strips in a colander and pour through boiling water from a kettle to blanch and soften. Pat the strips dry in kitchen paper and use them to line each oiled mould.

Pare and coarsely chop the remaining courgettes. Peel and chop the onion. Strip the leaves from the tarragon sprigs. Heat the oil in a 25 cm (10 in) frying-pan, add the onion and soften over a low heat. Add the courgettes, cover and cook gently until barely tender – about 10 minutes. Draw off the heat, stir in the tarragon leaves, then cool.

Turn the ricotta into a food processor bowl. Add the eggs and process for a moment. Add the courgette mixture, breadcrumbs, a seasoning of salt and milled pepper and the Parmesan. Cover and, using the pulse switch, blend to a coarse purée. Turn the mixture into the moulds and turn the edges of the courgette strips in over the filling.

Set the moulds in a large roasting tin and add boiling water to come 2.5 cm (1 in) up the sides of the moulds. Cover the tin with kitchen foil, tucking it in around the rim. Bake for 35–40 minutes until set. Leave until cold, then loosen the sides and unmould. Arrange the courgette and tarragon moulds on a serving platter. Add a few tarragon leaves to the dressing and spoon this over the moulds. Add folds of Parma ham if using.

Vegetable salad with honey dressing

The ingredients should be seasonal and can be all your own choice.

*250 g (9 oz) new baby
  carrots*
6 young courgettes
*175–225 g (6–8 oz) shelled
  broad beans or peas*
4–6 sticks green celery
½ cucumber
2 bunches spring onions
*2 x 400 g tin artichoke
  hearts*
2 tablespoons sunflower seeds
*2–3 tablespoons flatleaf
  parsley, coarsely chopped*
2 tablespoons snipped chives

For the dressing

2 tablespoons lemon juice
2 tablespoons clear honey
2 tablespoons olive oil
Salt and freshly milled pepper

Trim the stalk ends of the carrots, and add the carrots to a pan of boiling salted water. Simmer for 6–8 minutes or until barely tender. Rub or scrape off any skins. Leave tiny carrots whole, otherwise cut them lengthways at a slant. Don't peel courgettes if they're young and thin-skinned; slice them thinly into a colander and blanch with boiling water. Plunge them into cold water to preserve the colour, drain and press dry in kitchen paper. Add broad beans or peas to a pan of boiling salted water, cook for 2–3 minutes and drain. Pop the beans out of their skins. Combine the carrots, courgettes and broad beans in a large bowl.

Rinse the celery sticks, then snap and pull the halves apart to remove the strings. Shred the sticks with a knife. Pare the cucumber, cut in half lengthways and scoop out seeds. Then cut the pieces lengthways and dice. Wash and trim the spring onions, then chop the white part and some of the stems. Add the celery, cucumber and spring onions to the bowl. Drain the artichokes, rinse and cut the hearts in quarters. Add to the salad along with the sunflower seeds, parsley and chives. Toss the ingredients. Cover and refrigerate the salad. Combine the dressing ingredients with salt and milled pepper. Mix well, pour over the salad and toss.

Wine recommendations

As this is a celebration, best start with some bubbles. Blanc de blancs champagne – the type that's made entirely from Chardonnay – makes a wonderful apéritif, but for a less expensive alternative, try one of the increasingly good champagne-method sparkling wines from South Africa or Australia. Then move on to either a rosé wine from southern France or central Europe to go with the salmon, or, better still, a lightly chilled, midweight red made from Pinot Noir. Other red options might be a *cru* Beaujolais such as Fleurie or Chénas, or Dolcetto from the Italian region of Piedmont. Ice-cream is best left to its own devices, as its temperature tends to strip the subtleties out of wine.

Nutmeg ice-cream

The quantities here are for ease of mixing and freezing – and just right for an ice-cream maker. You will need to make it twice to serve twelve.

300 ml (10 fl oz) single cream
100 g (4 oz) unrefined golden caster sugar
4 egg yolks
Pinch salt
2 teaspoons freshly grated nutmeg
300 ml (10 fl oz) double cream
Muscovado sugar for sprinkling

Warm the cream in a pan. In a bowl cream the sugar and egg yolks until smooth and light, adding a pinch of salt. Stir in the warm cream. Return to the pan and stir over a moderate heat for 4–5 minutes, until the custard is smooth and creamy – do not boil. Draw off the heat and add the nutmeg. Stir to blend and turn into a bowl. Cool, then chill for 2–3 hours.

Whip the double cream to a soft consistency and fold into the custard. Turn the mixture into a container and freeze until firm (turn sides to middle and stir as the mixture hardens) – about 3 hours. Or freeze in an ice-cream maker – about 20 minutes. Store in a covered 1 litre (1¾ pint) container in the freezer. Transfer to the refrigerator 30–40 minutes before serving. Sprinkle with the sugar to serve.

Katie's tip

This is real ice-cream, made using a custard with egg yolks. I make my custard in a pan, stirring all the time without boiling – when the mixture is hotter than you can bear on the back of your hand, the custard is cooked; take the pan off the heat and pour into a cold bowl. Stir to prevent a skin forming. It will thicken up beautifully when cold.

PARTY PIECES

For a drinks party you want a luxury line-up of nibbles that are eye-catching, light and easy to eat with fingers. These can be prepared ahead of time and need only a bit of last-minute touching-up or reheating before guests arrive. I find that people are slow to help themselves to food at drinks parties so, instead of laying out everything beforehand, I bring in a succession of items from the kitchen, one dish at a time, so there's always something new on the go.

Food at drinks parties should be no more than two-bite-sized. Aim to hand around six to eight varieties for a two-hour party. The kind of recipe you can make as a whole and then cut up, is always labour-saving. My puff pastry palmiers with a black olive tapenade, and cheese sablés are both easy to prepare and slice up into dozens.

A yoghurt and ginger marinade flavours the chicken satays; and to serve them, for a bit of fun, I colour the cocktail sticks by soaking them in hot water with a teaspoon of turmeric, then drying them – they quickly take the bright yellow colour. The idea of classic foods in miniature is always a hit, such as the mini Yorkshire puddings with a beef and horseradish topping (you could use the same batter with a tiny cocktail sausage added to make mini toad in the hole). For Thai prawn wraps, to save time use ready-made Chinese pancakes to wrap around chilli prawns.

At the end bring on something sweet such as tiny lemon tarts, or my chocolate dip with kumquats and physalis. It's a subtle and very acceptable way of letting guests know the show is nearly over!

The day before

Prepare and bake puff pastry palmiers with tapenade. Make cheese sablé dough and refrigerate. Marinate ginger chicken.

In the morning

Bake mini Yorkshire puddings. Grill or pan-fry steaks. Bake cheese sablés with goats' cheese and walnut topping. Marinate prawns and shred salad ingredients for Thai prawn wraps. Make chocolate dip.

2 hours before

Finish mini Yorkshire puddings with rare beef. Grill and spear ginger chicken satays. Assemble Thai prawn wraps.

Last minute

Pop palmiers in oven to crisp up.

Puff pastry palmiers with tapenade

If I had just a few friends dropping in for drinks, this is the savoury nibble
I would choose to make – it's quick and easy.

1 x 375 g pack fresh ready-rolled puff pastry, or 340 g pack frozen puff pastry, thawed
Flour for dusting
165 g jar of tapenade

On a lightly floured work surface, roll the puff pastry into an oblong about 38 cm (15 in) wide by 30 cm (12 in) deep. Straighten the edges with a knife and prick the pastry all over with a fork. Cut the strip lengthways down the centre to make two strips about 18 cm (7 in) wide. Spread the centre of one pastry strip with 1–2 tablespoons of the tapenade. Fold both long sides in so that they almost meet in the middle. Pat down firmly. Spread the folded pastry with tapenade on one side of the strip only. Fold the uncovered pastry half over on to the covered side, to create a narrow strip four layers deep. Repeat with the second pastry strip. Chill to allow the pastry to firm up.

Heat the oven to 200°C/400°F/Gas Mark 6. With a sharp knife, cut each piece of pastry into strips 1 cm (½ in) across – you will get about 30 palmiers from each piece, all showing the layers of tapenade inside. Arrange on wetted baking trays, placing the pieces cut sides against the tray, not too close together. Pinch each one at the open end to keep the shape. Put in the heated oven for 10 minutes, then flip over and return to the oven for a further 2–3 minutes, or until golden. Transfer to a cooling tray.

Before serving, tip these into a roasting tin and give them 3–4 minutes in a hot oven to crisp up.

Cheese sablés with goats' cheese and walnuts

Omit the cheese and walnut topping and this sablé dough will make delicious plain cheese biscuits.

175 g (6 oz) plain flour
Salt and freshly milled pepper
100 g (4 oz) butter, cut into
  pieces
50 g (2 oz) Parmesan, grated
1 egg yolk

For the topping

1 egg white
50 g (2 oz) chopped walnuts
100 g (4 oz) goats' cheese

Put the flour and seasoning in a food processor bowl. Add the butter and whiz into coarse crumbs. Add the Parmesan and whiz to mix. Combine the egg yolk with 1 tablespoon of cold water and add this with the motor running – when the dough begins to cling, stop the machine. Turn the dough on to a floured surface and knead once or twice to remove the cracks. Shape into a fat roll about 4 cm (1½ in) in diameter. Wrap in cling film, twist the ends like a cracker and chill until firm.

Heat the oven to 190°C/375°F/Gas Mark 5. With a sharp knife, cut the dough in 5 mm (¼ in) thick slices and place on greased baking trays: you will get about 36, so bake in batches. Lightly beat the egg white with a fork to break it up. Use it to brush each pastry biscuit, then sprinkle with the chopped walnuts and crumbly bits of goats' cheese. Place in the preheated oven for 10–12 minutes or until golden. Transfer to a wire rack and leave until cool.

Ginger chicken satays

A yoghurt marinade makes chicken pieces very tender. For serving with drinks, spear a couple of bite-sized pieces of chicken on each stick.

4 skinned chicken breasts

For the marinade
150 ml (5 fl oz) natural yoghurt
1 teaspoon garam masala
½ teaspoon turmeric
1 teaspoon light muscovado sugar
2.5 cm (1 in) fresh ginger, grated
1 tablespoon lemon juice

Trim the chicken fillets, and cut each one lengthways and then across into bite-sized pieces – you should get about 12 pieces from each one.

In a mixing bowl combine the yoghurt, garam masala, turmeric, sugar and grated fresh ginger. Add the lemon juice and mix well. Add the chicken pieces, and stir the mixture to coat them. Cover and marinate for at least 4 hours.

Heat the grill to moderately hot and set the grill rack about 7.5 cm (3 in) from the heat source. With a slotted spoon, lift the chicken pieces from the marinade and spread in a shallow baking dish. Set directly under the heated grill and cook for 10–12 minutes. Stir up the chicken pieces, turning them over as they cook. Allow to cool. Then spear 2 pieces of chicken for each cocktail stick (you'll need around 40).

Thai prawn wraps

Chinese pancakes make delicious wraps for finger foods.

200 g (7 oz) tiger prawns, cooked and peeled
1–2 tablespoons Thai fish sauce
2 bunches spring onions
½ cucumber
2 packets Chinese-style pancakes
Hot chilli (not pepper) sauce

Marinate the tiger prawns in the fish sauce for 1 hour in the refrigerator. Trim the spring onions, then shred lengthways in slivers. Cut up the cucumber into sticks.

Unwrap the Chinese pancakes and keep a stack covered with damp muslin while you're working to prevent them drying out. Take 1–2 pancakes at a time and smear all over with sweet chilli sauce, which flavours them and keeps them moist. Cut each pancake in half. Fold in the cut edges about 5 mm (¼ in). Position a tiger prawn, cucumber sticks and spring onion shreds in a bundle and roll up the pancake. Stack on a serving platter.

Mini Yorkshire puddings with rare beef and horseradish

If making mini Yorkshire puddings is not for you, perch slivers of rare roast beef with a dash of the horseradish and crème fraîche on pieces of firm-textured wholemeal soda or rye bread.

100 g (4 oz) plain flour
Pinch salt
2 eggs
225 ml (7½ fl oz) mixed
  milk and water or
  skimmed milk
Oil for greasing

For the topping
200 ml tub crème fraîche
1–2 teaspoons horseradish
  relish
2 beef fillet steaks

Sift the flour and salt into a mixing bowl, make a well in the centre and break in the eggs. Add the mixed milk and water or skimmed milk. Stir the eggs and liquid from the centre, drawing in the flour from the sides of the bowl, and mix to a smooth batter. Chill for at least 1 hour.

Heat the oven to 220°C/425°F/Gas Mark 7. Generously oil two 12-cup mini-muffin trays. Place them in the heated oven for 6–8 minutes until they're really hot. Stir the batter and pour into each cup, no more than half full. Return to the oven immediately and bake for 10–15 minutes or until well risen, crisp and golden. Give the tin a sharp tap to loosen the puddings and turn out. Repeat until the batter is used up – it is enough for about 30 puddings. Allow them to cool.

Combine the crème fraîche and horseradish relish to taste. Grill or pan-fry the steaks – 6 minutes for rare and 8–10 minutes for medium. Turn steaks once only, halfway through the cooking time. Let them cool.

To serve, top each mini Yorkshire pudding with a spoonful of horseradish and thin slices of the rare beef.

Wine recommendations

This festive spread is best accompanied by light dry whites and fizz. Nothing gets people into the party spirit quite like a glass of bubbly. The lighter styles of champagne, such as blanc de blancs, are particularly useful in this context, but there are some wonderful wines being made under the auspices of the big-name champagne houses themselves in California, Australia and New Zealand. Pink fizz from any of those regions is also an appealing party wine, but be sure to choose a dry one. If you're serving a still white as well, choose something that's easy to drink and won't exhaust the palates of your guests after one or two glasses. Italian Pinot Grigio, Alsace Pinot Blanc or an unoaked Chardonnay from southern France or Hungary will be much appreciated.

Chocolate dip with kumquats and physalis

The tangy orange-coloured fruits are perfect for dipping. Serve small
bowls of chocolate dip with kumquats cut in half and speared with a
cocktail stick, and physalis with the papery petals folded back.

*150 g bar Continental dark
    plain chocolate, broken into
    pieces*
300 ml (10 fl oz) milk
Vanilla pod (optional)
3 egg yolks
50 g (2 oz) caster sugar
1 tablespoon cornflour
Pinch salt
25 g (1 oz) butter

For dipping

*2–3 x 100 g (4 oz) packs
    physalis*
200 g (7 oz) kumquats

Place the chocolate pieces into a bowl that fits snugly over a
pan of hot (not boiling) water and stir occasionally until melted.
Warm the milk and vanilla pod, if using, in a pan until hot.
Remove from the heat and infuse the milk for 5 minutes. Remove
the vanilla pod.

In a mixing bowl combine the egg yolks, sugar, cornflour and
salt until smooth. Stir in the hot infused milk, blend well and
strain back into the rinsed-out pan. Place over a low heat and stir
continuously until the custard boils: the cornflour stops the
mixture separating. Remove from the heat and stir in the butter
and melted chocolate. Pour into a bowl and allow to cool, stirring
occasionally to prevent a skin forming.

A GRAND SPREAD

menu for 10

- PEAR AND BLUE CHEESE CROSTINI
- SPICED RICE WITH SMOKED FISH
- BAKED FENNEL WITH PARMESAN
- WATERCRESS, CHICORY AND WALNUT SALAD
- CHAMPAGNE JELLY WITH GOLD LEAF

A supper party for a special occasion calls for glamour – the beauty of this high-style spread is that most of the preparation can be done before guests arrive so you can keep your cool. Your friends will be chatting and enjoying themselves, so start with something simple that won't interrupt conversation. Served hot and handed round on paper napkins, my pear and blue cheese crostini are stylish toast slices that will keep everyone's hunger pangs at bay.

I have often cooked smoked haddock kedgeree for a party – guests always love it. My recipe for spiced rice with smoked fish is an upmarket version, enriched with smoked salmon and decorated with smoked mussels in their shells. Experience has taught me that it's quite easy to get everything ready for the kedgeree in stages, then at the last minute add the stock to the rice and cook. When

timeplan

The day before
Bake the crostini bases.
Make the champagne jellies.

In the morning
Prepare spiced rice; poach
then flake haddock and
snip salmon into ribbons.
Cook fennel ready for
baking. Prepare salad leaves
and chill in a polythene
bag. Toast and chop
walnuts for salad and make
dressing. Slice pears for
crostini into lemon juice.

Last minute
Toss salad in dressing.
Assemble and cook crostini.
Make curry sauce.
Add stock to spiced rice
and cook. Bake fennel.

it's a larger than usual quantity, the rice may take longer to come to a simmer but the moment it does you've got only 15 minutes to wait before serving this delicious steaming dish. You need a pan large enough to cook the rice and still leave room for folding in the smoked fish, so beg, borrow or steal a stainless steel preserving pan – it makes life so much easier. To go with the kedgeree, I suggest a simple recipe for fennel braised to a tender sweetness and a bright green, crunchy salad of watercress and chicory to pep up the taste buds.

End with a spectacular dessert of champagne jellies set with edible gold leaf. This looks wonderful served in champagne flutes but, if you don't have enough of them for champagne *and* dessert, opt for slim tulip-shaped white wine glasses instead – the tall glasses really show off the gold leaf.

Pear and blue cheese crostini

Pears are usually sold hard and unripe. Keep them at room temperature for five to six days and they will ripen perfectly.

1 ready-to-bake ciabatta loaf
4–6 tablespoons olive oil
6 fresh ripe pears
Juice 2 lemons
300 g (11 oz) blue cheese –
  Roquefort, dolcelatte or
  Stilton
Paprika

Heat the oven to 200°C/400°F/Gas Mark 6. Cut the ciabatta into 1 cm (½ in) thick slices for the crostini (you should get at least 20 slices) and place them on oiled baking trays. Using a pastry brush, coat the uppermost side of the bread slices with olive oil. Place in the oven and bake for 8–10 minutes until pale golden and crunchy – there's no need to turn the slices as the side against the baking tray will brown at the same time. Let the crostini slices cool. Quarter and core the pears, and peel them if you don't care for the skin. Slice lengthways into slivers and turn in lemon juice to keep them white.

Place the crostini slices in neat rows on ungreased baking trays. Arrange the pear slices on the crostini, then top with slivers or crumbly bits of blue cheese. Place in an oven heated to 180°C/350°F/Gas Mark 4 for 5–6 minutes or until the cheese is melted (or grill until the cheese is bubbling). Dust with paprika and serve straightaway off the trays, placing on paper napkins.

Spiced rice with smoked fish

The mildest curry sauce keeps this flavoursome mixture moist.

The smoked salmon is a luxurious extra.

2 medium onions
100 g (4 oz) butter
1 tablespoon fennel seeds
1 tablespoon yellow mustard
  seeds
700 g (1½ lb) basmati rice
1.5 kg (3 lb) smoked haddock
  fillet
300 ml (10 fl oz) milk
250 g (9 oz) smoked salmon
6–8 saffron strands
1.75 litres (3 pints) vegetable
  stock
Salt and freshly milled pepper
300 ml (10 fl oz) double
  cream
2 teaspoons curry paste
450 g (1 lb) smoked mussels
  in shells (these are cooked
  and ready to eat)
Juice 1 lemon

Peel, halve and very finely slice the onions. Melt the butter in a 3–4 litre (5–7 pint) flameproof casserole or a wide pan with a lid. Add the fennel and mustard seeds and heat, stirring until the mustard seeds begin to pop. Stir in the sliced onion, cover and cook gently for 6–8 minutes or until the onion is soft and translucent. Add the rice and stir until it is coated with butter. Sauté gently for 2–3 minutes, then remove the pan from the heat.

Cut the haddock into manageable pieces and place in a large pan. Add the milk and enough water to cover the fish, then put the lid on the pan and poach gently until the fish is just cooked – about 10 minutes. Remove the fish from the liquid and leave until cool enough to handle. Peel off the skin, discard any rogue fish bones and break the flesh into large flakes. Cut the smoked salmon into ribbons, and set aside. *2 min. is enough.*

Add the saffron to the hot vegetable stock and infuse for 5 minutes. Taste the stock and season if necessary. Place the pan of rice over a moderate heat and stir until it is hot and sizzling again. Add the saffron stock to the rice, stir and bring to a simmer. Lower the heat, cover with the pan lid (or with kitchen foil tucked around the pan rim) and cook gently for 15 minutes until the rice grains are tender and the stock is absorbed. Remove from the heat and keep covered – the rice will retain the heat perfectly for a further 10–15 minutes. *20 is better. Depends on the kind of rice.*

Combine the cream and curry paste in a small pan and heat. Fold the haddock and the smoked mussels into the spiced rice. Add the lemon juice and mix through – do this in a large bowl if necessary. Pile the mixture on to one or two heated serving platters. Top with the ribbons of smoked salmon, spoon over the curry sauce and serve.

Baked fennel with Parmesan

Slow gentle cooking tenderizes the fennel and sweetens the flavour;

raisins make an interesting addition.

5 fennel bulbs
75 g (3 oz) butter
2 tablespoons olive oil
Salt and freshly milled pepper
75 g (3 oz) seedless raisins
50 g (2 oz) grated Parmesan

Trim the base and tops of each fennel bulb and remove any coarse outer covering. Cut each bulb in half lengthways and cut away the core. Place the halves cut side down on a chopping board and slice thinly lengthways.

Melt 25 g (1 oz) butter with 1 tablespoon of olive oil in a 25 cm (10 in) frying-pan (with a lid) and add half the fennel. Cover with the lid and let the fennel sweat over a low heat until it is tender when pierced with a knife tip – about 20 minutes. Remove the lid, raise the heat and sauté, turning the slices over until they are lightly browned – about 5 minutes. Season the mixture with salt and pepper. Turn the fennel into a 2 litre (3½ pint) buttered gratin or baking dish. Repeat with the rest of the fennel. Sprinkle with the raisins and Parmesan and dot with the remaining butter.

Heat the oven to 180°C/350°F/Gas Mark 4. Place the dish of fennel in the oven and bake for 15–20 minutes – then serve.

7 mins is best.

I think might overcook a delicate vegetable.
Try braising it in butter with mint & 1 tab. water

Watercress, chicory and walnut salad

Walnut oil adds a delicious nutty flavour to this colourful, crunchy salad.

100 g (4 oz) walnut pieces
1 teaspoon walnut oil
4 x 85 g packs watercress
4–6 firm white heads of
    chicory
Salt and freshly milled pepper

For the dressing

1 tablespoon red wine vinegar
Salt and freshly milled pepper
4 tablespoons olive oil
1 teaspoon walnut oil

Heat the oven to 180°C/350°F/Gas Mark 4. Toss the walnuts in the walnut oil and bake for 5–6 minutes or until lightly toasted. Leave to cool, then chop the walnuts finely.

Pick over the watercress, separating leafy stems and discarding thick stalks. Slice the chicory heads in half lengthways and cut out the core. Then cut across the leaves in 2.5 cm (1 in) thick slices and separate out the layers. Combine the dressing ingredients.

Tip the watercress and chicory into large salad bowls and season with salt and pepper. Toss the leaves with the dressing and walnuts, then serve.

Champagne jelly with gold leaf

This recipe will fill ten glasses, allowing about 140 ml (5 fl oz) in each.

Measure the volume of a glass you plan to use to ensure even portions.

1 x 75 cl bottle dry
champagne or sparkling
wine
7 sheets fine leaf gelatine
175 g (6 oz) caster sugar
2–3 pieces pared orange rind
3 tablespoons Cointreau
2 sheets edible gold leaf

Pour the champagne into a medium mixing bowl and let the bubbles subside. Place the sheets of gelatine in a bowl (they fit more easily if they are cut in half), cover with cold water and leave to soak.

Pour 600 ml (1 pint) water into a pan, then add the sugar and orange rind. Stir over a low heat to dissolve the sugar, and bring almost to a simmer. Remove from the heat. Squeeze the gelatine to remove excess water, then add it to the pan and stir to dissolve. Leave the gelatine mixture to cool to room temperature, then discard the orange rind. Stir the gelatine into the champagne, then add the Cointreau.

Line a few large roasting or baking tins (they must fit in your refrigerator) with a folded tea cloth. Lay a ridge of crumpled newspaper lengthways down the centre. Place champagne flutes or tulip-shaped glasses in the tins, with the bowl of the glasses on the newspaper ridge so that the first addition of jelly will set on a slope. Spoon 2–3 tablespoons of jelly into each glass, then refrigerate for about an hour until set. Keep the remaining jelly at room temperature.

Carefully open out the delicate gold leaf. With the tip of a small pointed knife, break the gold leaf into small pieces. Use the tip of a fine paintbrush to transfer the pieces of gold leaf on to the set jelly – about 2–4 in each glass. Use the paintbrush to coat each piece of leaf with some of the remaining jelly then return the glasses to the refrigerator for 20 minutes to fix the gold leaf in position. Stand the glasses upright and fill with the remaining jelly. Refrigerate to set. An alternative to gold leaf could be halved, seeded black grapes.

Katie's tip
To order edible gold leaf at £2.95 per sheet or £18.75 for 10 sheets, plus postage and packing, contact Squires Kitchen (telephone: 01252 711749). Allow five working days for delivery.

Wine recommendations

Assertively flavoured white wines with perhaps a hint of residual sugar are the racing certainties here. The blue cheese on the crostini needs some counterbalancing sweetness (especially if you've opted to use Roquefort) and smoked fish can take it too. Gewürztraminer or Pinot Gris from Alsace are sound choices, and are full of diverting aromatic personality, or you might try a Spätlese Riesling from the Rheingau or Pfalz regions of Germany. Otherwise, an oaked Sauvignon from California or Bordeaux would work equally well. With the champagne jellies, it would be churlish to drink anything other than champagne. And with the luxurious glitter of gold leaf on show, go for the best that the budget will allow.

Index by course/ingredient

Soups and possible starters
Asparagus with chopped eggs – serves 8
(the slimmer asparagus stems in a mustard dressing) 80
Butternut squash and apple soup – serves 6
(a warming soup with croutons) 106
Chick pea and black olive pâté – serves 4
(serve with warmed pitta bread) 98
Crunchy marinated vegetables – serves 4–6
(tender-crisp steamed vegetables in a marinade) 98
Cucumber and mint dip – serves 4
(a fresh-tasting yoghurt mixture) 72
Mixed leaves with bacon and white Stilton – serves 6
(with the crunch of grilled bacon and croutons) 116
Roasted aubergine dip – serves 4
(an aubergine purée with black olives) 72
Smoked haddock pâté – serves 6
(this one is buzzed in the blender) 56
Spinach salad with hot bacon dressing – serves 8
(needs last minute preparation) 14
Taramasalata on rye bread – serves 6
(home-made is paler and altogether more delicious) 133
Tomato tarts with basil – serves 6
(using ready-rolled puff pastry – these look terrific) 30
Twice-baked spinach soufflés – serves 10
(can partly prepare the day before) 46
Warm scallop salad – serves 8
(stir-fried scallops with a colourful, sweet chilli dressing) 22

Fish and seafood
Fresh spaghetti with chilli sauce and tiger prawns – serves 6
(fresh pasta with an unusually good combination of flavours) 74
Italian-style fresh tuna salad – serves 6
(a colourful mix of seared tuna, capers and black olives) 134
Mediterranean baked sea bass – serves 8
(foil-baked and served with garlic mayonnaise) 81
Monkfish gumbo – serves 6
(a fish stew with rice to serve as a main dish) 114
Peppered tiger prawns with dill mayonnaise – serves 6
(offer as finger food – these prawns are for dipping) 124
Provençal roast monkfish – serves 6
(a classic but simple way to cook monkfish) 31
Salmon in puff pastry – serves 8
(crisp pastry makes a lovely contrast to the delicate texture of salmon) 38–9
Seared salmon in mustard and dill – serves 12
(individual portions served in a pretty dressing) 158

Smoked fish canapés – serves 8
(to serve with a glass of wine) 64
Spiced rice with smoked fish – serves 10
(an up-market version of kedgeree, with smoked salmon) 175
Taramasalata on rye bread – serves 6
(home-made is paler and altogether more delicious) 133
Tiger prawns with chilli aioli – serves 6
(skewered prawns to cook on the barbecue) 142
Warm scallop salad – serves 8
(stir-fried scallops with a colourful, sweet chilli dressing) 20, 22

Poultry and game
Braised pheasant with wild mushrooms – serves 8
(rich flavoured braise using pheasant breasts) 15
Corn-fed chicken with lemon and shallots – serves 6
(tangy with lemon and spiced with a cinnamon stick) 57
Duck salad with spiced pears and sweet soy dressing – serves 6
(cold duck is always delicious – the spiced pears are a bonus) 126
Honey-glazed duck in grapefruit and ginger sauce – serves 10
(roasted duck breast fillets with a tangy fruit flavour) 48
Marinated chicken in lemon and tarragon dressing – serves 8
(vinaigrette makes a change from the usual mayonnaise dressings) 65

Meat
Butterflied leg of lamb – serves 8
(boned leg of lamb for the barbecue) 99
Herb-marinated lamb skewers – serves 12
(Mediterranean-style skewers served with lemon) 150
Honey-glazed roast lamb with honey mint sauce – serves 8
(a traditional roast with a delicious mint sauce) 90
Mixed brochettes – serves 10
(individual pork, prawn, halloumi and potato skewers for the barbecue) 140–2
Peppered beef fillet – serves 8
(flash-roasted and served cut in thick slices) 23
Pork satays – serves 6
(marinated in a soy sauce dressing – for the barbecue) 140
Spiced pork loin steaks with prunes – serves 6
(caramelized onions add to the rich flavour) 108

Vegetables
Baked fennel with Parmesan – serves 10
(slow cooking brings out the sweet taste

of fennel) 177
Boulangère potatoes – serves 8
(sliced and oven-cooked in stock) 24
Braised leeks with hazelnuts – serves 8
(with a delicious toasted-nut flavour) 92
Courgette and tarragon moulds – serves 6
(serve with slices of Parma ham for a main course) 161
Courgette terrine – serves 8
(served cut in slices – suitable for vegetarians) 82
Dauphinoise potatoes – serves 8
(the classic recipe using cream) 92
French-style peas – serves 10
(cooked with salad leaves, spring onions and herbs) 49
Garlic and olive oil mash – serves 6
(leave the garlic out if you prefer) 58
Glazed carrots – serves 6
(a butter and sugar glaze emphasizes their natural sweetness) 58–9
Halloumi brochettes – serves 6
(skewered cubes of cheese with cherry tomatoes – for the barbecue) 140
Hot beetroot with butter and black pepper – serves 8
(serve with any game dish) 17
Hot vegetable platter – serves 8
(hot vegetables served with a vinaigrette or melted butter) 40–1
Mustard-glazed onions – serves 8
(small onions in a tangy butter glaze) 24
Pot-roasted new potatoes – serves 10
(oven cooked, then seasoned with sea salt and milled pepper) 49
Roasted aubergine with pesto – serves 8
(thick chunks of aubergine with basil pesto topping) 102
Skewered potatoes – serves 6
(par-cooked, then fixed on satay sticks – for the barbecue) 141
Spinach moulds – serves 6
(individual moulds made using a creamed spinach mixture) 32–3
Stir-fried green cabbage – serves 6
(bright green and fresh tasting) 108
Stuffed mushrooms with Parmesan – serves 4
(serve as a main dish for vegetarians) 93
Watercress sauce – serves 8
(spoon over any hot poached salmon or trout) 40

Pasta, grains and pulses
American wild rice and nut pilaff – serves 8
(oven-cooked, just fork through and serve) 17
Bulgar salad with fruit and nuts – serves 12
(includes dried apricots, lemon and almonds) 160
Buttered fresh noodles with walnuts – serves 6
(replace the walnuts with chopped fresh herbs, if preferred) 109

Index